METHODS
A JOURNAL OF ACTING PEDAGOGY

Volume 3, 2017
Pace University Press

Copyright © 2017
Pace University Press
41 Park Row
New York, NY 10038

All rights reserved
Printed in the United States of America

ISBN: 978-1-935625-22-3
ISSN: 2471-5905

Member

Council of Editors of Learned Journals

∞ ™ The paper used in this publication meets the minimum requirements of American National Standard for Information Sciences—Permanence of Paper for printed Library Materials

ANSI Z39.48—1984.

METHODS
A JOURNAL OF ACTING PEDAGOGY

EDITORS

SENIOR EDITOR
Ruis Woertendyke — Pace University

ASSOCIATE EDITOR
Charles Grimes — University of North Carolina, Wilmington

PRODUCTION EDITOR
Laurence Ruth — Pace University

EDITORIAL BOARD

Alicia Tafoya	Our Lady of the Lake University; Northwest Vista College
Dr. Lee Evans	Pace University
Dr. David Krasner	Dean College
Bara Swain	Urban Stages
Lilah Shreeve	Pace University
Leigh Woods	University of Michigan
Robin Post	University of North Carolina, Wilmington
Amy Guerin	University of Alabama
Dennis Schebetta	University of Pittsburgh
Jenn Calvano	University of Louisville

Note From the Editor

I remember turning into the drive-through lane at my bank some years ago and being stopped 100 feet from the bank by the instructions, "Please put your bank business in the container, close the container, drop it into the air-tube, and wait for the container to return with your receipt." I thought, even then, that it won't be long before we'll be banking without even seeing a human being. Little did I realize that that was just the beginning. Now we can see a couple eating dinner and texting each other at one table and watch an entire family on their separate phones at another. I hear people brag about having 5,000 friends on Facebook though they've seldom seen or talked to them. It's this kind of isolated technological community that has become our reality and it is this reality that makes theater so important and necessary.

The theater has become one of the last vestiges of instructive human behavior. We can watch cultural mores, ethics, morals, and practices of countries all around the world. We can observe more than a hundred generations of social conduct, humor, family difficulties, laws, love, and marriage. We are able to connect ourselves to thousands of years of human history. *The Oresteia* of Aeschylus has guided our sense of justice, Sophocles' *Oedipus Rex* has become part of our psychology, and *Romeo and Juliet* has come to define eternal love. The vast history of theater has helped us to define our lives.

Film, television, tablets, smartphones, Facebook, Twitter, LinkedIn, laptops, Netflix, and the rest of our cyber world does not bring us closer or make us better understand ourselves or each other. Our announced Facebook status is small talk and more often than not, connected to media. We are reaching a stage in our society where experience of life is inferior to experience with the computer; the Internet has become our playground.

Culturally, we need the theater to keep us aware of ourselves, our mores, and our responsibilities. We need to witness the pain and truth of O'Neill's *A Long Day's Journey into Night* and Williams' *The Glass Menagerie* to help us understand our own pain and truth.

These great plays give us the rite of passage, something we all need: the right to become ourselves. In the theater we can see who we are. David Mamet and Neil LaBute show us our cowardice and sexism while Ibsen lays out our struggle with justice for women, health, money, and duty. Chekhov and Beckett confront our impotence while Peter Weiss reflects our inhumanity. And what can we say about Shakespeare who confronted racism, anti-Semitism, sibling rivalry, magic, revenge, and love four hundred years ago? Edward Albee and Ping Chong give us portraits of the outsiders, the others, while A. R. Gurney chronicles the white Anglo-Saxon Protestants and August Wilson tells us the stories of African Americans. These plays are our lives. There is something and someone for each of us. All of us.

Many a modern person looks to films as a replacement for theater, as an equal or even a superior platform for behavior. However, there are several issues with this theory, not the least of which is the perpetual past in which a film lives. The conflicts we see are edited to serve the purposes of the director and the reactions between players are not spontaneous even though they may have been in one of the many takes. No matter how the audience responds, the film, the moment will not change. Even with the advent of 3D made common, there is no depth of humanity in film; there is only the height and width of the human figure. Made up of light and sound, film presents us as sixteen feet tall, and with close-ups, heads that are six feet wide. These overblown images of our species that are the mainstay of film are a distortion of the human figure and require a more subtle approach to behavior than in normal life.

We have all seen Neil Simon's work on both film and television. Perhaps it is that fact that leads so many of us to view him as a shallow writer. But he is not shallow: He is a humorist, and somehow we are led to believe humor lacks the depth of seriousness. But, we must not forget that the comic is the registration of a grievance, and in our desensitized community, humor is an important path to the serious. Simon has spent a lifetime registering grievances and doing

Editor's Note

so with great popularity. Then, what play has not been thinned down by the screen: Odets' *Golden Boy*, Crowley's *The Boys in the Band*, *The Laramie Project* by Moises Kaufman, *Romeo and Juliet*, *Othello*, *A Midsummer Night's Dream* or *Hamlet*? Perhaps Marshall McLuhan is right in saying the medium is the message, not the content. Films make us big and powerful with a deluded sense of universality. The only true advantage of filmed plays is the possibility of star power. However, the theater has a power that no film can possibly duplicate: the power of the living, breathing actor.

Thespis is generally considered the first actor to step outside the chorus and play an individual role. He was accused by Solon, a Greek legislator, of teaching the public to tell stories and to lie because of the nature of the actor's art. Thespis explained that it was not a lie because it was play. Of course we know that the people of the world did not need to be taught to lie by an actor and we have come to understand, as Picasso said, that all art is "the lie that reveals a deeper truth."

The primary source of American acting is the method developed by Constantine Alexeiev whose stage name was Stanislavski. He tried Aaron Hill's ten facial gestures, Delsarte's postures and gestures, and many other techniques until June 22, 1897, when he met with director/teacher Vladimir Nemirovich-Danchenko to discuss the problems with the Russian theater. Through this discussion came the development of the Moscow Art Theater. The lack of the theater's initial success guided them towards *The Seagull* by Anton Chekhov which, in turn, guided them to a new approach to acting: psychological realism. It is this psychological realism that is our primary approach to acting on stage, in film, and serious television even in the twenty-first century. Interestingly enough, I attended the Moscow Art Theater in 2009 and could feel the power of this new form as it pulled the theater away from the presentational style that preceded it. At the same time, Stanislavski's method has not evolved in Moscow to the same degree it has in the United States. In Moscow, we can still see a kind of formal realism that has nearly disappeared in this country. And now we are moving away from psychological realism because our lives are moving into a world of technological reality. And the stage will keep us abreast of those changes.

So, what is it that gives the theater such a permanent power? What makes the living actor such a draw, such a greater teacher of humanity, more so than the recorded actor? It is the actual human being living in the same time and space as we are. It is watching actual men and women confronting life issues and overcoming or succumbing to them. Feeling pain and joy, fear and courage, love and hate, revenge and forgiveness, and all the emotions coming from living people, like us—people we can share our experience with, who can share their insights and interpretations, people who look like us and act like us—released.

The living theater becomes an experience shared by the actors and the audience. In 1982 I saw James Earl Jones playing Othello on the stage of the Winter Garden, that cavernous theater, and being completely moved by his almost naïve and unworldly portrayal of the great Moor. His tragic and elongated decision to suffocate Dianne Wiest's Desdemona sent me and the rest of the audience out weeping. When we left the theater, I could actually see moist spots of tears on shirts and blouses. In fact, I was so impressed that I invited two friends to join me to see the production later in the run. The second time through, the show was not as exciting: Christopher Plummer's Iago wasn't quite as malevolent and though Wiest was as innocent, Mr. Jones was playing with a bit too much effort and the audience was not quite with him. Clearly he felt that and he tried even harder to capture the audience. By the time he was contemplating the murder of Desdemona, the audience was giggling under its breath and my friends returned to their belief that *Othello* was truly a melodrama. I was disappointed. But now, more than thirty years later, I remember it clearly and so do my two friends. What we saw was not so much Othello, as the struggling James Earl Jones.

In the middle of February 1964, Beah Richards was rehearsing Sister Margaret in James Baldwin's *The Amen Corner* directed by Frank Silvera. She had just been cast to replace an actress who "wasn't working

Editor's Note

out" and had only two weeks to rehearse this long and difficult part. I worked the box office to pay for my acting lessons with Frank and when the show started I would go in to watch. The show opened on March 4, 1964, and on that night at a key emotional point of the play, Beah yelled "line" at the same volume and emotional level as the scene she was playing, and it was a moment of magic that made Beah's absolute professionalism so clear and thrilling. It was as though that was part of the script. I remember that "line" like it was yesterday. One night, Frank challenged me to watch the audience rather than Beah and I could not—she was too compelling and I'll never forget her performances: always alive, invested, truthful, and inspirational.

Many times in my life I heard the living theater's death knell. Its death was announced in the 1950s when television came into our lives and again in the 1960s with the beautifully filmed versions of Broadway musicals like *My Fair Lady* and *The Sound of Music*. Actually, I've heard it throughout my life.

Recently, Rocco Landesman, the one-time chair of the National Endowment for the Arts and a well-known Broadway producer, declared, "There are too many theaters. If there were fewer theaters, they'd have the resources to pay their artists more." His history as a Broadway producer seems to have limited his view. It is as though Broadway and the major regional theaters were the only valuable theaters in the country. The theater however is more than a business; it is an important part of our culture. There are more than 7,000 community theaters mounting 46,000 productions a year with an audience of 86 million and an annual budget of more than 980 million dollars. These facts alone speak to the importance theater has in our culture. And as I think about the death knells, I remember Ron Willis, one of my mentors, responding to these dire predictions by saying, "The theater will never die because people like you and me need to do theater and there will always be people like us. Theater is a part of our DNA." In fact, theater is a part of our cultural DNA and its value to our society is growing ever more important

—R.W.

TABLE OF CONTENTS

Author	ARTICLES	Page
Tracey Moore	Actor Training for the Digital Age	1
Jessie Mills	Practicing Guerilla Theater: Practical Tools and Exercises to Expand Performance and Theatricality	13
Adrienne Kapstein	A Multiplicity of Voices	25
Isaac Eddy	Theater of the Vulnerable: How Being a Blue Man for Twelve Years Taught Me about Acting, Directing, and Teaching	37
Cosmin Chivu	An Interview with Neil LaBute	56
Brian Hastert	How and Why to Teach Acting for Film, Television, Voice Overs, and Commercials	89
Jessie Mills	The Triangle Game: A Practical Exercise to Introduce and Build Skills in Commitment and Ensemble	103
Bara Swain	Casting a Ten-Minute Play Festival or Which Way to the Acting Pool?	111

HISTORY

Historical Document

Joseph Jefferson	From *The Autobiography of Joseph Jefferson*	123

BOOK REVIEWS

Suzanne Delle	*Cracking Shakespeare: A Hands-on Guide for Actors and Directors + Video* by Kelly Hunter. London: Bloomsbury Methuen Drama, 2015.	133
Matt Fotis	*Performing in Comedy: A Student's Guide* by Ian Angus Wilkie. London: Routledge, 2016.	137
Jenn Ariadne Calvano	*Actor Movement: Expression of the Physical Being* by Vanessa Ewan and Debbie Green. London: Bloomsbury, 2015.	141
Dennis Schebetta	*Roadblocks in Acting* by Rob Roznowski. London: Palgrave, 2017.	145
Leigh Woods	*A Director's Guide to Stanislavsky's Active Analysis* by James Thomas. London: Bloomsbury, 2016.	151
	Actioning—And How to Do It by Nick Moseley. London: Nick Hern Books, 2016	
Amy Guerin	*The Actor's Business Plan: A Career Guide for the Acting Life* by Jane Drake Brody. London: Bloomsbury Methuen Drama, 2015.	157
	The Thriving Artist: Saving and Investing for Performers, Artists, and the Stage & Film Industries by David Maurice Sharp. Burlington, MA; Abingdon, UK: Focal Press/ Taylor & Francis, 2015.	

Melissa Miller	*An Actor's Task: Engaging the Senses* by Baron Kelly. Indianapolis, IN: Hackett Publishing Company, 2015.	163
Ellen W. Kaplan	*Acting, Imaging, and the Unconscious* by Eric Morris. Los Angeles: Ermor Enterprises, 2015.	167
Jeffrey Toth and Charles Grimes	*Acting, Archetype, and Neuroscience: Superscenes for Rehearsal and Performance* by Jane Drake Brody. London: Routledge, 2017.	173
Amber Jaunai	*Black Acting Methods: Critical Approaches* by Sharrell D. Luckett and Tia M. Schaffer. London: Routledge, 2016.	181
	Notes on Contributors	187
	Call for Papers	193

Actor Training for the Digital Age

By Tracey Moore

For those of us who teach in college theater programs and who were trained in America during the late 20th century, the Stanislavski methodology is our bread and butter. It is still the primary technique used by most actor training programs. Meisner training, while growing in popularity, can be considered an offshoot of Stanislavski (Barfield). But in the next couple of years, colleges will welcome the first freshman cohort born exclusively in the 21st century. Due to societal and technological advances, this group, which I will refer to as Cohort 1, will have fundamentally different ideas of human behavior than acting students of the mid-20th century for whom Stanislavski was such a revelation. These students of Cohort 1 have had a unique experience of social interaction and may, in fact, have different brains (Carr 33). The question is: What adjustments to actor training do we need to make for them?

Nothing feels as good as a "ping," scientists tell us. Our brains receive a squirt of the neurotransmitter dopamine—the "feel good" chemical—any time our phone chimes to signal an incoming message or post (Weinschenk). The most susceptible have become addicted to their phone. This disorder has tentatively been given a name, "nomophobia": feeling bereft, anxious, awkward, and nervous if we are without it; waking up in the middle of the night to check for messages (Roberts). If this were heroin, the addiction might be more apparent. But because these behaviors don't interrupt functionality (in fact, being "always available" is the very definition of functionality!), we allow, and even expect it. But this addiction interrupts the life of an actor in the most fundamental way: eliminating the possibility for quiet reflection and imaginative mind-play (akin to daydreaming) essential to creativity (Jabr October) and the formation of character, and even interfering with the ability to read (Jabr April) or sleep (Grandner 1302).

Basic concentration is affected, too. Mid-twentieth-century Americans were familiar with continuous, sustained, full attention and focus on one thing. Those people born since 1995 engage in "continuous partial attention." This is not the same as multi-tasking, which combines one activity requiring minimal brain attention with another that requires more attention for the sake of efficiency, e.g., washing the dishes while talking on the phone. Continuous partial attention requires that the brain constantly shift from one thing to another. The motivation is not efficiency, but FOMO ("Fear of Missing Out"), so you need multiple awarenesses. If you watch television while surfing the Internet and texting, you are using continuous partial attention. To have a meaningful conversation in addition would not be productive or even possible. Repeatedly using your brain in this way can affect one's "ability to reflect, to make decisions, and to think creatively" (Stone). In short, our brains have changed as a result of online activity. Iain McGilchrist is a British psychiatrist and writer who studies the brain and society in a holistic way. In a recent interview, he said:

> What we experience, how we think, and what we do with our brains modifies the brain, by affecting synaptic growth and threshold, amongst other things: that modifies the likelihood of our brains responding to what they experience in a certain way. . . . That means that we are constantly exposed to numerous positive feedback loops. First, the more we think x now, the more we are likely to think x in the future. Second, the more we think x, the more we will build a world that expresses x, and the more we will experience x, and so the more we will think x, etc. (McGilchrist)

Body Postures

The way we use our bodies has changed as a result of technology, too. Electronic devices (primarily cellphones) require a repetitiveness of posture which can cause various kinds of physical ailments. A painful condition called "text neck" comes from having hands and arms in front of the body with the head downward, i.e., in the texting and swiping position. When a phone is not in use but is being held, the phone is normally clasped in one hand with fingers curved around the phone to support its weight. That requires various muscles (fingers, hand, wrist, forearm, bicep) to be continually active, and can result in arm or wrist pain. Many students walk while looking at their cellphones, which requires one arm be kept stationary, as opposed to walking with opposite arms swinging in "cross-lateral" movement. Cross-lateral movement, which occurs when arms and legs cross *over* from one side of the body to the other, is the basic action of walking. Theories hold that since the right side of the brain controls the left side of the body and vice versa, the whole brain "communicates" with itself when cross-lateral movement occurs (Cooper); preventing cross-lateral movement means preventing this brain activity. Because the head is tilted downward when students walk with their phones, the eyes are engaged in close or mid-range vision rather than the long-range sight that occurs when eyes are focused toward the horizon. Peripheral vision is less engaged, and step length and speed must be modified to avoid injury (Park). An actor's body is his or her instrument, so physical challenges in real life will inevitably affect onstage life.

Social Interactions

Much has been said about how technology is changing the nature of social interactions. In her book *Reclaiming Conversation*, Sherry Turkle suggests that college students, unaccustomed to face-to-face contact, may now actually "fear" conversation (34). Breaking off a relationship via text is now acceptable (Krueger). Today's college students struggle with eye contact. "Rich, messy, and demanding" relationships are made safer with the distance afforded by technology ("Flight from Conversation"). Unfortunately for theater students, rich, messy, and demanding is often what's called for in a play. Our new ability to edit a message before it is sent, to be represented by an avatar more attractive than our current selves, or to unfriend anyone whose point of view differs from our own: these actions serve to sanitize, distance, and protect us.

But, protect us from what? Clinical psychologist Sally Kuhlenschmidt explores college students' fears under the headings "What they don't talk about" and "What they are afraid to face." She suggests that while American college students of the mid-20th century grappled with sexual repression and emerged with more sexual freedom and more access to their emotions, today's college students are afraid of failure, of being cut off from parents, and of being criticized. They have trouble dealing with criticism because it is too hard to think about being bad, wrong, or unsuccessful (Kuhlenschmidt). Jean Twenge, writing in *Generation Me*, observed that failure itself is unthinkable to Millennials: "If you can dream it, you can be it" was the internalized watchword of the 1990s (77). The problem for actors is that failure (try again, fail again, fail better—to paraphrase Samuel Beckett) is intrinsic to creativity: you cannot have one without the other.

Cohort 1, having lived exclusively with modern technology, is likely to be susceptible to the problems noted above. If electronics are changing our students' brains and bodies, we must change the way we train students to be actors. Many of us teach the way we, ourselves, were trained. But with concentration, physical bodies, and brain activity altered so much in a single generation, it is not feasible to expect that millennials will handle theatrical material as previous generations did. Cohort 1's bodies and minds will be coming to Stanislavski differently. There may be the need for remedial training in concentration or coordination. If students cannot make eye contact, they cannot do scene work. If they cannot work with singular, focused concentration on a particular idea or piece of text, they cannot do a play. The acting classroom could be the antidote for many of the damages wrought by technology, but (a) that takes time away from teaching the craft and (b) it is doubtful that a few hours spent in a class will outweigh the remaining hours of the day spent engaged with technology. We all get what we practice.

A New Approach

In my own classroom, I have begun to approach things from a different angle. Recently, a colleague laughingly said, "Nowadays, we have to sneak up on our students!" (Hall) and I think he is correct. I have begun to use some "outside-in" methods and have turned to social science research for ideas.

Exercise 1

For a recent production of a play that required deep intimacy and physical trust between on-stage partners, I borrowed from the work of Dr. Arthur Aron, a psychologist who researches interpersonal relationships. Dr. Aron's original study was designed to explore whether intimacy could be created. He had several pairs of strangers (a male and a female) meet and ask each other approximately 36 questions divided into three groups that became progressively more personal, with periods of sustained eye contact between the groups of questions (Jones). After this study, two participants ended up marrying, and it was a sound byte that caught the attention of *The New York Times* (Catron). I had already been experimenting with "eye contact practice" in my beginning acting classroom and had seen the benefits, so I believed there was something of value here.

The play was made up of small two-person scenes, so I worked with each pair separately. I provided students with questions on strips of paper housed in an envelope that could be passed back and forth (partners should take turns asking the questions, but both people should answer each question). Since I was looking to build connection and intimacy but not necessarily "love," I modified the study's parameters. I used fewer questions in each group, and I began by having the students answer some questions as themselves before answering the questions as their characters would. Some examples of questions were, "When did you last sing to yourself?" or "What would constitute a perfect day?" (Aron 374). I adjusted the eye contact—shorter but more frequent time periods. (The scene partners for this play were male/female and male/male.) It should be noted that I also adjusted the parameters of the exercise because of time constraints: I wanted to give students enough time to cycle through the intimacy work with enough time afterwards to transition into scene work without feeling rushed. That meant that one entire night's rehearsal was devoted to this exercise for each set of partners.

I stepped in and out of the room to act as timer for the eye contact segments, to supply the next set of questions in a new envelope, and to make sure that no one was unduly uncomfortable with the work. But mostly, I left students alone—though I did peek through a window in the door. I observed the actors' body language and facial expressions change as the exercise progressed. Both male and female students relaxed and engaged in a wider variety of facial expressions (faces became less "tight") as the time wore on. They gradually became more emotional (more tears, more laughter), and both men and women gradually began to engage in intimacy behaviors (women touching their hair and necks, men leaning back in their chairs and raising arms overhead to push their chests forward) ("Flirting".) When we began rehearsing afterwards, the actors said they felt more comfortable with each other. Rehearsal of scenes that involved touching (which had been awkward before the exercise) now brought easy laughter and physical cooperation between scene partners.

As part of their pre-show warmup, students were encouraged to repeat portions of this exercise. In conversations after the show, students informally reported that these warmups made them feel more "connected" to each other on stage. I was not aware until after the show that students had devised their own intimacy exercises to use during warmups (slow dancing, embraces) as the run of the show went on.

Exercise 2

I have collected a number of old fashioned, black-and-white postcards and photographs of people from between 1890 to 1950.

I use these as well as postcard-sized prints of fine art works for an acting exercise based on the work of psychologist Paul Ekman, which holds that assuming a facial expression will lead to an emotional state related to that expression (Ekman). The pop-psychology version of this is to behave "as if" (Wiseman 11), which is not too far removed from Stanislavski's theory of the Magic If, but rather than trying to work from the inside-out (determining motivations, desires, relationships, and letting those dictate action), we begin with the externals.

Students choose a postcard or work of art that they feel contains the essence or likeness of the character they are exploring, and assume—down to the tiniest detail—the physical position of the person in the photo. They are required to hold this posture/facial expression/gesture for several minutes, and to explore how it is affecting them (pain, discomfort, freedom, openness, tightness, expansiveness, fear, etc.), and then begin to speak some text or a monologue spoken by their character. After holding that position for a while, I ask students to move to what would seem to be the next "logical" position or gesture—an outgrowth of the previous position. We spend time moving back and forth from the photo position to the new physicality and then add text.

To further develop a vocabulary of movement and physicality, one can create flashcards that dictate physical actions (examples might be to put both hands in front of you; touch both ears; put one hand above your head, the other on your face) and ask students to choose two or three, and put the flashcards face down. Students should establish their photo position, turn over one flashcard, and move from photo position into the new one dictated by the flashcard. The flashcard descriptors should be somewhat open ended: Although the card could say "touch both ears," it should give no further information about how to do it: Students could choose to grasp ear lobes, cover their ears, use pointer fingers to press the ears back, or cross their hands over the top of their heads and touch ears with opposite hands. After the first flashcard, point out the several ways a card might be interpreted so that students know they can enact these postures as their character might (so far, just the character in the picture). Then move on to flashcards two and three. The number of flashcards is flexible; I chose three as a starting point.

We continue to build the external aspect of the character by layering: choosing additional qualities or inspiration from other artwork, photos, gestures, and objects (I keep a box of broken children's toys for this purpose) and trying to translate visual or sensory stimuli into gesture or movement or action, and from there, into behavior and text. Obviously, as with any acting exercises, some students are more adept than others, but it is possible to fashion a character in this external way and eventually start to "live" through that behavior. Actor Johnny Depp has spoken about using imagery and external ideas to build film characters. For the character of Ichabod Crane, Depp said he combined "part teenage girl…and part Angela Lansbury" to come up with "Ichabod Crane: girl detective." For the character of Ed Wood, Depp talked about three stimuli: the "blind optimism" of Ronald Reagan, the enthusiasm of the Tin Man from *The Wizard of Oz*, and radio jockey Casey Kasem (Depp; Blitz, and Krasniewicz 97-98).

Exercise 3

Another outside-in exercise involves creating a large number of adjective flashcards (confused, awestruck, joyful, frightened, disgusted, ecstatic, etc.). Flash the cards at random at the rate of roughly one card per line or two at students working through a monologue. Ask that they immediately take on the feeling associated with the word—not in an attempt to illustrate the word so that viewers could guess it, but in a way that takes the actor over completely—face, body, voice, etc. Whatever happens as a result of the word should be considered ideal: there should be no attempt to engineer things so that a particular adjective elicits a certain behavior from the actor, or aligns with a particular moment in the text. In fact, opposition is wonderful (a sad monologue with an ecstatic moment or two occurs in every Chekhov play). When you have finished, talk about what was surprising or weird, and which of the events the actor wants to retain. On a more macro level, i.e., for a whole scene, use the "Oblique Strategies" flashcards created by composer Brian Eno to change things up. These are a series of koans/suggestions subtitled "Worthwhile Dilemmas" which seek not to address a creative problem directly, but to put the creator in a different relationship to the creative activity. An example might be a single word, like "Cascades," or the phrase "Be less critical more often," or the query, "How would you have done it?" Other flashcards, like brainstorming cards designed originally for corporate situations, can also be adapted for use.

Exercise 4

Wesley Balk was the artistic director of the Minnesota Opera for two decades, and was known for his work with opera and musical theater performers. He is the author of several books, including *The Complete Singer-Actor: Training for Music Theater*, which contains many good inside-out exercises originally designed for songs or scenes (176). His legacy continues with the Wesley Balk Opera / Music Theater Institute in Minneapolis. The training there includes an acting exercise referred to as OOPS/UBU. (These acronyms stand for "One and Only Perfect Sound" and "Unusual But Useful" sounds.) This is an exercise used for singers that I have modified for use with actors.

There are two ways to use this exercise. First, establish an imaginary horizontal line that is about 3 feet in front of the actor, at about waist height. This represents a continuum. Next, select a quality or emotion that is relevant to the text that you want the actor to amplify or explore. At one end of the horizontal line is the number 1, which indicates a rather weak level of the quality / emotion. At the other end is the highest level there is (10). Using your hand, slide along the continuum from 1 to 10, and ask the actor to embody that emotion or quality as they speak the text, increasing from a 4 or 5 or 6 on the "line," with the highest level going so far as to include the loss of text altogether. An example might be the exploration of grief. The continuum in this case might progress from light sadness or melancholy all the way to keening. You can backtrack occasionally (going from 1 to 5 and back to 3), but avoid big jumps like 1 to 10, which are unsettling for the actor. The actor should speak text as you explore the continuum, but allow for various noises (Unusual But Useful sounds), laughter, sighs, and so on, if they occur.

A second use of this imaginary continuum is to place one emotion, quality, characteristic, or action (e.g., the emotion of joy) at one end, and a seemingly opposite idea (sadness) on the other. You can also explore two different qualities—fear and attraction, or hesitancy and lightheartedness—as long as they are relevant for the text. As the actor begins to work the monologue or chunk of text, slide your hand very slowly along the imaginary continuum as the actor speaks so she or he experiences the journey from one idea to another; or use two hands to bring both, disparate ends toward a 50 / 50 point in the middle that would represent the perfect mix of joy / grief or fear / attraction. Just as with the adjective flashcards, the point is not for viewers to guess or define what they are seeing, but for the actor to completely and suddenly embody whatever comes to mind, and to let it affect the text and him or herself.

Conclusion

With all of these exercises, success will depend in part on the actor. If the student actor is willing, brave, and open, then the activities will land deeply within her or him. Outside-in approaches, just like inside-out, require a level of commitment from the actor without which nothing will result. These exercises, if done fully, should lead actors to character and relationship-building in a way that doesn't require them to sit quietly in still thought, something that many millennials find difficult to do. The partnered building of intimacy and eye contact, the physical behavior borrowed from pictures and artwork, and the fast changes of the flashcard emotions will supply new and stimulating ways of approaching character while also addressing the digitally-induced issues mentioned above.

Professor Sergei Tcherkasski from the St. Petersburg State Theatre Arts Academy, speaking at the S-Word Conference in England (S-Word), said: "If we agree that [the] Stanislavski system is a research system—it is not a system of answers, but a system of questions—then new steps in physiology or psychology will bring new laws, new elements, new prompts for actors." This is the philosophy I hold: that the "System" is flexible enough to accommodate new approaches, and that it is our responsibility as teachers to design them. Stanislavski could never have imagined the advent of technology that we have today, just as our students could not imagine life without it.

Works Cited

Aron, Arthur, et al. "The Experimental Generation of Interpersonal Closeness: A Procedure and Some Preliminary Findings." *Personality and Social Psychology Bulletin*, vol. 23, no. 4, 1997, pp. 363-377. Print.

Balk, H. Wesley. *The Complete Singer-Actor: Training for Music Theater*, 2nd ed., Minneapolis: Minnesota UP, 1985. Print.

Barfield, June. "There is no such thing as Meisner, Adler, Strasberg, or Hagen Technique or Method." *Backstage* magazine, 18 April 2017. Web. 29 April 2017. <http:// www.backstage.com/advice-for-actors/backstage-experts/ there-no-such-thing-meisner-adler-strasberg-or-hagen-technique-or-method>.

Blitz, Michael, and Louise Krasniewicz. *Johnny Depp: A Biography*. Westport, Connecticut: Greenwood Publishing Group, 2008. Print.

Carr, Nicholas. *The Shallows: How the Internet Is Changing the Way We Think, Read, and Remember*. New York: Norton, 2010. Print.

Catron, Mandy Len. "To Fall in Love With Anyone, Do This." *The New York Times*, 9 January 2015. Web. 2 May 2017. <http://www.nytimes.com/2015/01/11/fashion/ modern-love-to-fall-in-love-with-anyone-do-this.html>.

Cooper, Greg. "Cross-Lateral Exercises." *Livestrong / Sports and Fitness / Fitness / Shoulder Exercises*, 20 June 2011. Web. 2 May 2017. <http://www.livestrong.com/ article/474736-cross-lateral-exercises>.

Depp, Johnny. "Inside the Actor's Studio." *Dailymotion*. n.d. Web. 2 May 2017. <http://www. dailymotion.com/video/xzx0zx_johnny-depp-inside-the-actors-studio_shortfilms>.

Ekman, Paul, et al. "Voluntary Smiling Changes Regional Brain Activity." *Psychological Science*, vol. 4, no. 5, 1993, pp. 342-345. Print.

"Flirting Body Language." psychologia.co. n.d. Web. 2 May 2017. <http://psychologia.co/ flirting-body-language>.

Grandner, Michael, et al. "The Use of Technology at Night: Impact on Sleep and Health." *Journal of Clinical Sleep Medicine*, vol. 9, no. 12, 2013, pp. 1301-02. Web. 29 April 2017.

Hall, Doug. Conversation at Music Theatre Educators' Alliance New York Conference. 7 January 2017.

Jabr, Ferris. "The Reading Brain in the Digital Age: The Science of Paper versus Screens." *Scientific American*, 11 April 2013. Web. 30 April 2017. <http://www.scientificamerican.com/article/reading-paper-screens>.

———. "Why Your Brain Needs More Downtime." *Scientific American*, 15 October 2013. Web. 2 May 2017. <httpwww.scientificamerican.com/article/mental-downtime>.

Jones, Daniel. "The 36 Questions That Lead to Love." *The New York Times / Modern Love*, 9 January 2015. Web. May 2017. <http//www.nytimes.com/2015/01/11/fashion/no-37-big-wedding-or-small.html>.

Krueger, Alyson. "New Dating Rules: Break-Ups Through Text OK, Playing Hard to Get Not OK." *Forbes / Lifestyle*, 9 March 2014. Web. 2 May 2017. <http://www.forbes.com/sites/alysonkrueger/2014/03/09/you-can-break-up-with-a-girlfriend-through-text-and-other-new-dating-norms/#24d122c914bd>.

Kuhlenschmidt, Sally. Interview at Western Kentucky University. March 2014.

McGilchrist, Ian. "Interview with Iain McGilchrist." *Frontier Psychiatrist*. Web. April 2017. <http://frontierpsychiatrist.co.uk/interview-with-iain-mcgilchrist>.

Park, Jaeheung. "Synthesis of natural arm swing motion in human bipedal walking," *Journal of Biomechanics*, vol. 41, no. 7, 2008, pp. 1417-1426. Print.

Roberts, James A., et al. "The invisible addiction: Cell-phone activities and addiction among male and female college students." *Journal of Behavioral Addictions*, vol. 3 number 4, 2014, pp. 254–265. Print.

Stone, Linda. "Continuous Partial Attention." Web. 2 May 2017. <http://lindastone.net/qa/continuous-partial-attention>.

Tcherkasski, Sergei. "Forward—to early Stanislavsky! or Reconstruction of Actor Training at the First Studio of the Moscow Art Theatre." The S Word: Stanislavski and the future of Acting Conference. 19 March 2016. Web. 10 January 2017. <http://www.theatrefutures.org.uk/stanislavski-centre>.

Turkle, Sherry. "The Flight from Conversation." *The New York Times, Sunday Review*, 21 April 2012. Web. 2 May 2017. <http://www.nytimes.com/2012/04/22/opinion/sunday/the-flight-from-conversation.html>.

———. *Reclaiming Conversation: The Power of Talk in a Digital Age*. New York: Penguin, 2015. Print.

Twenge, Jean. *Generation Me*. New York: Simon and Schuster, 2006. Print.

Weinschenk, Susan. "Why We're All Addicted to Texts, Twitter and Google." *Psychology Today*, 11 September 2012. Web. 2 May 2017. <http://www.psychologytoday.com/blog/brain-wise/201209/why-were-all-addicted-texts-twitter-and-google>.

Wiseman, Richard. *The As If Principle: The Radically New Approach to Changing Your Life*. New York: Simon and Schuster, 2013. Print.

Practicing Guerilla Theater: Practical Tools and Exercises to Expand Performance and Theatricality
by Jessie Mills

Performances outside of the walls of a Theater (with a capital "T") can be thrilling, dangerous even. Live, site-specific performance that reacts directly to our times and incorporates spontaneity is one that dares, evokes, and often defies. Tracing back to theatrical forms such as Commedia dell'arte, politically infused theater often utilized improvisation to respond to a live audience, to bend material to suit the needs of immediate news, and to evade censorship (Crohn Schmitt 226).

In the midst of social unrest in the 1960s and early 70s, a new mode of spontaneous, political theater arose in America: Guerrilla Theater. Richard Schechner defines Guerrilla Theater as "symbolic action. It is called 'guerrilla' because some of its structures have been adapted from guerrilla warfare—simplicity of tactics, mobility, small bands, pressure at the points of greatest weakness, surprise" (Davis 163).

Simplicity, mobility, and surprise are essential to the form. Indeed, these qualities allow guerrilla artists to plan and execute quickly. In response to the brutal Kent State shootings in 1970, Schechner, along with his colleagues and students, were able to devise a production, *The Kent State Massacre*, which was performed the very next morning. This performance led to the quick and focused development of a series of performances around New York illuminating "the obvious message: the war was home" ("Guerrilla Theatre" 164).

In R.G. Davis' seminal article on Guerrilla Theater (written almost exactly fifty years ago), he argued:

> This society, our society—America, U.S.A.—is chock-full o' ennui. Distracted by superficial values, and without a sense of humanness, we let machines rule; it is easier to kill from a B-52 than to choke every Viet Cong. No one feels any guilt,

> not even the poor fool dropping the bombs. Theatre has contributed to alienation by presenting a performer who is hemmed in from costume to head. He too is a number in a basket, a character "type," and he trains his "instrument" to take orders. (130)

Indeed, history and art are cyclical. Our contemporary political climate seems ripe for theater that interrupts and challenges the status quo. Students of Guerrilla Theater must not be only, as Jill Dolan so eloquently articulates, "scholar/artists but *citizen*/scholar/artists," who do not "participate in unselfreflexive nationalism but . . . use art and research, aesthetics and intellect to participate in a civic conversation about what 'America' is and what it does" (518).

This work utilizes different muscles than traditional theater training. It begins with critical inquiries into the macro- and microstructures of the commonplace and marries such analyses to aesthetic and movement. As Davis illuminates, "what makes this type of theatre difficult? Content, style, and external effects or repercussions" (131).

Guerrilla Theater, at its core, is a vessel for activism. In process and practices, it questions power structures and enacts civic engagement. In some ways, this type of theater cannot be taught in a traditional sense and, indeed, is messier than most training. Davis cautions us that, "the first steps are necessarily hectic and loosely ordered. Few long-range plans can be made" (135).

In this article, I will outline three "hectic and loosely ordered" introductory exercises to guide students toward the practice of Guerrilla Theater. Each exercise focuses on one facet of Davis's trio of difficulties (style, content, and external effects) while taking all three into account. The first exercise aims to identify elements of our social script and to use theatricality to interrupt the quotidian; it emphasizes style. The second exercise requires students to investigate issues that affect them; it prioritizes content. The final exercise demands that students understand how a piece of Guerrilla Theater may affect an audience; it underlines external effect.

Exercise 1: The Social Script

> "Start with people, not actors."
> — R.G. Davis

This exercise begins with a cursory foray into sociology. I will often distribute excerpts from Erving Goffman's essential text, *The Presentation of Self in Everyday Life,* or begin class with a few of Goffman's more germane quotes on the board (perhaps defining "front," and "repertoire of actions"). I almost always write out Goffman's notion that, "[i]n short, we all act better than we know how" (73-74).

Once students have grappled with a basic understanding of performance of the self in a variety of settings and dynamics, I ask for an example action to use as the basis for an in-class performance. I ask that these examples contain two qualities: first, that the action is a small, repeatable, and a singular gesture or interpersonal exchange. Second, that their peers use the chosen gesture in common practice. For the sake of this description, we'll use "the handshake."

Next, I gather students into pairs (or groups) and have them write the stage directions (i.e., the nonverbal steps) for a handshake. This is not an exercise in playwriting; there are to be no given circumstances. Rather, students must delineate the exact physical minutia (or "story") of the gesture or exchange. For instance:

Person A stands facing Person B with arms at side.

Person B stands facing Person A with arms at side.

Person A bends right arm at the elbow, at a ninety-degree angle, with fingers extended and palm open to Person A's left.

Person B bends right arm at the elbow, at a ninety-degree angle, with fingers extended and palm open to Person B's left.

Persons A and B simultaneously extend forearms until respective open palms are touching.

Person A and Person B encircle fingers so as to grip the bottom, fleshy area of partner's palm.

> While maintaining grip, Person A and Person B's hands move up and down, together, one to three times.
> Person A releases grip.
> Person B releases grip. Persons A and B both retract hands, returning to original position.

The process of detailing a performed social action naturally abstracts it, highlighting its more theatrical qualities.

Next, I have groups exchange stage directions and "perform" the actions exactly as written. This typically results in a series of surrealist comedy acts. After students perform the full set of stage directions, we discuss what seemed consistent, what was missed, and what felt ambiguous. In the example above, for instance, there are no specific details for the position of the body beyond the right hand. Are the feet together or shoulder-width apart? Should partners make eye contact, and if so, for how long? Are knees locked or bent? We also discuss, as often comes up, the theatrical nature of societal mores.

This in-class exercise can be repeated using a number of examples of varying difficulty. For instance, a class might start with a simple gesture ("the wink") and move up to dynamic and complex exchanges ("the flirtation across a room"). With each example, students will become more capable of dissecting and recreating an exact gesture, as well as more aware of the abstracted minutia of each action.

These stage directions, purposefully, often mirror performance "scripts" from the Happenings, a "pan-artistic phenomena" (Kaprow, "On Happenings" 281) that was rooted in an obsession with "the space and objects of our everyday life, either our bodies, clothes, rooms, or, if need be, the vastness of Forty-second Street" ("The Legacy" 187). As students' skills are sharpened in the art of theatricalizing the quotidian, I introduce articles from Allan Kaprow and his contemporaries. Richard Schechner further contextualizes the art form as, "[opposed to Abstract Expressionism, the Happenings] choose everyday objects and people for material and destroy the figurative by confronting it, not by distorting or ignoring it" ("Happenings" 232). Indeed, this first exercise explicitly confronts the everyday.

I also introduce students to lighter fare that showcase theatrical interruptions of or confrontations with the status quo. The popular group, Improv Everywhere, most famous for their annual "No Pants Subway Rides," claims that they "[aim] to surprise and delight random strangers through positive pranks, or 'missions'" (improveverywhere.com). Additional examples include commercialized flash mobs (via companies such as bookaflashmob.com) and viral videos attached to advertising campaigns. It is important to understand how the intention behind the interruption affects the aesthetic of performance.

Depending on the length of the class and choice of the instructor/students, this exercise can remain a single activity (one to two weeks) or become a full unit (three to four weeks). In the case of a full unit, I end with a site-specific performance. I ask students to choose a space on or near campus where a gesture or series of actions occurs in conjunction with the space. We then create a performance text, much in the vein of our earlier stage directions, to confront the social script of that space.

An example from a past class utilized the social script of a campus cafeteria. Students first identified one specific element of the social script: the use of a tray in the cafeteria. They analyzed the utility within the script of the tray: a stabilizing element; a marker of "ownership," or the boundaries around an individual's food; a system of transportation; a symbol of egalitarianism; a symbol of homogeny. Students then devised their performance text in an effort to confront some of those embedded meanings:

15 performers enter the cafeteria in a uniform line, with Performer 1 at the head of the line.
One at a time, each performer takes one tray from the tray rack, holding it perpendicular to his or her torso.
Each performer moves to a separate table with an open seat.
Each performer completes the following series of actions three times:

1. Softly places tray upside down on table
2. Turns tray up ninety degrees so that it is perpendicular to the table. Holds for 30 seconds
3. Slams tray down so that it is right side up

After the series has been completed, each performer picks up the tray and stands, once again holding the tray perpendicular to her or his torso.

Performers cross to the center of the cafeteria, until all performers create a standing circle with trays inward.

Using the right hand, each performer passes his or her tray to the performer to the right.

Performers complete this action three times.

Performer 1 begins walking to the dishwashing conveyor belt.

15 performers place their empty (and clean) trays, one at a time, onto the conveyor belt and exit the cafeteria in a uniform line.

While, in this case, students chose to create a performance around the same object or gesture, there is also value in devising separate tracks. Students might link tracks or create a series of contained, isolated vignettes.

The purpose of this unit is not to extend the principles of Guerrilla Theater into Happenings or vice versa. In fact, Davis warns against Guerrilla Theater "turning...to twisted naturalistic symbolism, pop art, camp, or happenings for the chic" (132). Rather, this exercise should attune students to the plethora of social scripts around them and highlight how theatre can be employed as interruption. It should prime students to understand how to use theater within as a space, rather than against it.

Afterward, a conversation about aesthetic, intentionality, and "audience" response should follow. Did this performance hew closer to that of the Happenings or that of a Positive Prank? What was its style? Moreover, in the world of Guerrilla Theater, how might we discuss this performance in terms of activism?

Exercise 2: Accessing Activism

> "For those who like their art pure of social issues, I must say—F*** ***! buddy, theatre IS a social entity."
> — R.G. Davis

Theater is an inherently political act. The performance of text or story is one that privileges a specific voice and point of view; it is an art form that relies on complicated modes of representation. However, theater is not solely political. Davis firmly reminds us that in Guerrilla Theater:

> [if] the content is too immediate, the art is newsworthy and, like today's newspaper, will line tomorrow's garbage pail. If the content is devious, symbolic, or academically suggestive, the public will refuse to see it, because their minds have been flattened by television and dull jobs. (131)

How, then, do we find content that is neither too immediate nor too symbolic? How do we help our students respond to a movement rather than a moment? There are, undoubtedly, many approaches an instructor can take. In my classroom, I conduct a two- to three-week activity that I call the "empathy exercise." The forced perspective of empathy, in my experience, helps to curtail content that is "too immediate."

First, I guide students in creating an operational (i.e., active rather than passive) definition for empathy. I help to steer students away from conflating empathy with pity and encourage a definition that is inclusive in nature. I ask students to consider how one might *cultivate* empathy or how they might teach it as a skill. I then ask students to practice their empathy and come to class with a short video or story that activated their empathic response. They should be prepared to show or read the story and "teach" classmates how to empathize with those portrayed in the narrative. This exercise typically takes two to three full class periods.

Next, as Guerrilla Theater is inherently tied to locality, I ask students to repeat the assignment but, this time, using stories within their personal spheres, ideally from peers on campus. It cannot be their story or that of another student in the classroom, and it must have occurred within six months of the assignment. Again, students should be prepared to relay their found story and "teach" their classmates. An instructor should plan for another two to three full class periods to complete this second exercise.

Where empathic perspective curbs flashy content, the immediacy and proximity of these stories similarly restricts empty symbolism. The underlying themes and issues in these latter accounts will ultimately create the basis for our performance(s). Students may spend up to another week discussing which issues and themes stood out for them and may form as many performance groups as desired. Students need not be evenly distributed among the groups and there may be groups of one; the most important ingredient to Guerrilla Theater is passion.

Having developed the appropriate modes of empathy toward a set of themes and issues, the question remains: in taking theater outside of its walls, what are the "external repercussions"?

Exercise 3: Intentionality in Interruption

> "Go where the people are—street corners, vacant lots, or parks... [b]egin the show by playing music, do exercise warm-ups, play and sing, [parade] around the area, attract an audience. Keep the length of the show under an hour, moving swiftly, and adapting easily to accidents, dogs, bells, children... keep improving and learning even after the show opens. The show should close better than it began."
> — R.G. Davis

Guerrilla Theater is, by definition, *theater*, and therefore needs an audience. In Davis's eyes, to keep an audience (specifically one that has not paid for tickets in advance and consciously carved out a period of time to watch a production), actors need to make a piece worth watching.

Schechner takes Davis's assertion one step further. He argues that performers must understand and prepare for the nuances in "friendly, neutral, unfriendly, and hostile places / audiences" ("Guerrilla Theatre" 166). Moreover, Schechner recommends that performers "be ready to split quickly after an action in an unfriendly place; or, on the other hand, be ready to stick around and rap for a long time in a friendly place" (166).

I encourage one step further: that performers commit to intentionality behind their interruption, thereby presupposing how each type of place / audience will receive their performance. To address our intentionality, my classroom came up with a makeshift four-quadrant grid, where our x-axis represented "amusement" and the y-axis represented "activism." Amusement, in our case, addressed how much the performance focused on pleasing/entertaining an audience, where the left quadrants focused more on the interest of performers themselves and the right quadrants focused on the interests of the audience. Activism, in our case, represented the type and use of the content. The upper quadrants skewed toward critical evaluations of social issues, while the lower quadrants skewed toward lighthearted fare.

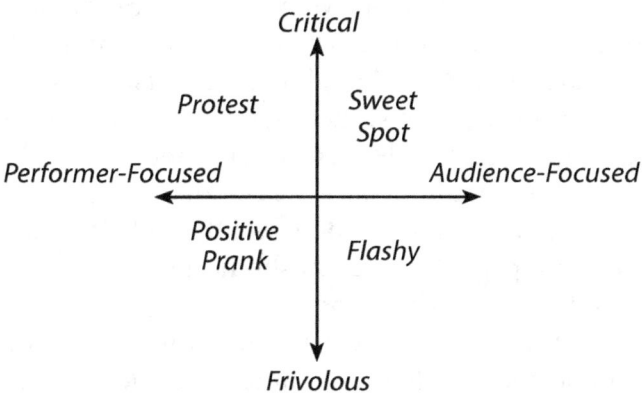

In our breakdown, we estimated the type of performance and audience interaction that would evolve within each quadrant.

The top left quadrant, where performers focused on their interests ahead of their audience's reception, and where serious societal critiques were launched, would likely hew more closely to that of a protest. As such, we should expect some instances of unfriendly (and even hostile) audiences. The bottom left quadrant hosts experiences such as the "positive prank." We can still expect some unfriendly audience members here, though likely more irritated than angry. The bottom right quadrant might be a flashy, outdoor production. We can expect our most neutral and our friendliest audiences here. The upper right quadrant (the sweet spot, in Davis's outlook) would both entrance an audience *and* extend social critiques. We would likely expect a combination of friendly and unfriendly audiences, but it felt less likely that we would encounter hostile spaces.

There are, undoubtedly, a myriad of categorizations, as well as ways to define axes. This is just one system I used with students to classify and strategize around Guerrilla Theater. Creating a similar (or completely new) model should take no more than one class period. In our case, we used this quadrant system as a means for feedback and preparation as students prepared their final performances.

To strengthen our understanding of our created system, I also assigned each student to find one video of an untraditional, site-specific performance. I asked that each student bring less than five minutes of material to class, though the piece itself did not need to be under five minutes—the student could present a few excerpts. As a group, we watched each performance and assigned it a location within the four quadrants. By the end of each presentation, the quadrants were filled with titled dots and the full class felt that they were on the same page. Instructors should expect this assignment to take one to two full class periods.

Understanding the type of engagement for which these performances aim and the likelihood of audience response was essential in the process of creation. In interrupting the social script, one invariably creates a new social contract and it is to the benefit of all—performers and audience member alike—to enter into that contract with thought and consideration.

Conclusion

These exercises merely scratch the surface of Guerrilla Theater and are designed to begin exploration and development within the art form. Furthermore, they are a useful set of activities to address Davis's trio of style, content, and external repercussions. Additional exercises are begging to be loosely, hectically developed. And, certainly, now is the time for development.

On May 13, 2016, the WhoWhatWhy podcast interviewed L. M. Bogad, author of *Electoral Guerrilla Theatre: Radical Ridicule and Social Movements* and a performance studies professor of theater and dance at the University of California at Davis. Bogad championed the use of theatricality and socio-drama in contemporary political protests. Bogad cautioned that, "older forms of political protest may . . . have less impact because they kind of get swallowed up by this entertainment culture that we have, and it's easier to ignore" (00:2:24-00:02:36). Bogad encouraged heightened creativity and imagery, noting that, the more compelling the image, the more likely that it will be reproduced in and by our media.

Of course, we must not forget Davis's warning to think beyond content that will line our wastebaskets alongside yesterday's newspaper. Rather, Bogad calls for a new infusion of energy into theatrical protest: "sometimes when there's more repression, and satire has to work harder in an almost clandestine way, it's harder to do and it's more dangerous, but there's a higher bar for work that's going to get out there" (00:06:22-00:06:40). As we enter another cycle of Americans "chock-full o' ennui...and without a sense of humanness," the tools of Guerrilla Theater remain ever valuable.

Works Cited

"About Improv Everywhere." *Improv Everywhere*. Improv Everywhere Productions, Inc., 30 May 2016. Web. 31 May 2017. <http://www.improveverywhere.com>

Crohn Schmitt, Natalie. "Improvisation in the Commedia dell'Arte in its Golden Age: Why, What, How." *Renaissance Drama*, vol. 38, 2010, pp. 225-249. Print.

Davis, R. G. "Guerrilla Theatre." *The Tulane Drama Review*, vol. 10, no. 4, 1966, pp. 130–136. Print.

Dolan, Jill. "The Polemic and Potential of Theatre Studies and Performance." *The Sage Handbook of Performance Studies*, edited by Soyini D. Madison and Judith Hamera, Thousand Oaks: Sage Publications, Inc., 2006, pp. 508-526. Print.

Goffman, Erving. *The Presentation of Self in Everyday Life*. Random House, 1959. Print

Kaprow, Allan. "The Legacy of Jackson Pollock." 1958. Reading Abstract. *Expressionism: Context and Critique,* edited by Ellen G. Landau, Yale UP, 2005, pp. 181–187. Print.

Kaprow, Allan, and Mimsy Lee. "On Happenings." *The Tulane Drama Review*, vol. 10, no. 4, 1966, pp. 281–283. Print.

Schechner, Richard. "Guerrilla Theatre: May 1970." *The Drama Review*: TDR, vol. 14, no. 3, 1970, pp. 163–168. Print.

———. "Happenings." *The Tulane Drama Review*, vol. 10, no. 2, 1965, pp. 229–232. Print.

Schechtman, Jeff. "Protest Theater In An Age Of Entertainment Politics?" *WhoWhatWhy*. Audio blog post.

A Multiplicity of Voices

by Adrienne Kapstein

What is Devising?

Devising, theatre-making, performance making, collective creation, play building and *generative artistry* are all terms used to describe a process which places the creative efforts equally in the hands of a collective of artists and embraces the joint construction and crafting of original work. What unites all of these monikers is the emphasis on process. And yet it is crucial to note that there is no singular process — no system — of how to devise. Collectively created work is project-specific, company-specific, specific to each and every moment within the creative development period. Such a praxis fundamentally disrupts any conventional hierarchies and re-orders any systematized mode of development. A traditional script is not the starting point and text is not necessarily privileged as the primary theatrical language being utilized. "Everyone in the room is a creator of the piece" (Rinear 13) and any theatrical element (sound, movement, music, design, multi-media, language) can take the lead and determine the direction of the work.

An analog analogy for a collaborative mode of creation is a photograph being developed in a darkroom. Different parts of the image come into focus at different times: a shape is revealed in one corner, something materializes in the foreground, a form appears in the background. It is iterative, accumulative, unpredictable, and yet all the separate elements work in concert with one another towards building a whole. In a devised process, design and technical elements are no longer reserved for meetings prior to rehearsals nor relegated to tech week at the end. A piece of music can be the instigation for creative inquiry; a physical gesture can inspire decisions on the nature of the theatrical world; a costume piece can act as an entry point into the creation of a character where in a traditional process more value might be placed on what a character says.

Artists drawn to working in this way are curious not just as to what story is being told but how the story is told. They are interested in using all the poetic devices the stage has to offer (Kaufman 24) and in utilizing the different 'languages' of theatre to drive the storytelling. As Moisés Kaufman said in "What is Devised Theatre?", a roundtable conversation with John Collins, Eric Dyer, Winter Miller moderated by Rinne Groff in *The Dramatist* (Mar/Apr 2015), devising can be looked at as "writing performance as opposed to writing text" (24). It is important to note however that devised work does not preclude using text or incorporating a playwright in the process. Elevator Repair Service, for example, often places text at the center of their work. *Gatz* was the staging of every single word in Fitzgerald's novel, *The Great Gatsby*, and their 2015 show, *Fondly, Collette Richland*, was devised in collaboration with playwright, Sybil Kempson (New York Theatre Workshop).

Although the term "devised theatre" may be relatively new in the United States, the practice of devising in American theatre is not new at all. The Living Theatre, Joseph Chaikin's Open Theater, Bread and Puppet Theater, Mabou Mines, and the ever active and forward-looking Wooster Group are all examples of long-standing American artists pushing against pre-existing models and methods and creating work collectively. The following generation of ensembles such as Pig Iron Theatre Company, Elevator Repair Service, the TEAM, and the Rude Mechs have now been around long enough to become staples of the experimental theatre scene and are regular exports to Europe, where their work is even more widely embraced than in the United States.

Devising has taken root in the U.S. however, and over the past twenty years there has been a proliferation in the number of not-for-profit ensemble theatre companies (Novick 2011) with many of these groups creating work in endless iterations of what devising can look like. An increasing number of new shows created via an ensemble-driven process are also making their way onto mainstream stages. Recent examples of commercially successful productions that originated in processes where the cast and creative team were equal contributors to the creation of the work, at least in their early developmental stages, include *Peter and the Starcatcher* and *Natasha, Pierre & the Great Comet of 1812*, as well as U. K. transfers of the National Theatre's *War Horse* and Complicité's *The Encounter*. Newly established support from institutions like the Public Theater's Devised Theater Initiative created in 2014 and the Drama League's Impact Residency launched in 2016 are explicitly geared toward ensemble-generated work and illustrate how this mode of production—fundamentally counter to the dominant, playwright driven model in the U. S.—is finally starting to be recognized and legitimized.

One of the reasons it has taken so long for this alternative mode of creation to take hold in mainstream American regional theatre is that it requires significantly more time in development, more people in the room, and is therefore more expensive. It also raises difficult questions of ownership and authorship and therefore of payment, rights, and royalties. If the work is created collectively, who does it belong to, how are the artists credited, and how are people paid?

American colleges and universities are also reflecting the influence and presence of ensemble driven, collectively created work with the inclusion of courses that give students the opportunity to make their own theatre and the recent emergence of undergraduate degree programs specifically dedicated to training students to generate original material. Recent examples include Pace University's own International Performance Ensemble BA program launched in 2012 and Boston Conservatory's Contemporary Performance BFA program launched in 2015. The BFA (and MFA) theater programs at Sarah Lawrence College, however, have incorporated devising practices since the late 1980s under the leadership of Shirley Kaplan (Kaplan 2017) and today it is still strongly committed to a cross-disciplinary collaborative training, producing "actors who write; directors who act; theatre makers who create their own projects". (https://www.sarahlawrence.edu/undergraduate/arts/theatre/)

The Pedagogy of Collaboration

With its arrival in academia, the question arises, how does one teach devising? How can students learn to become generative, as opposed to interpretative, artists? If the work does not begin with a pre-existing script, what tools and techniques do actors need to make the work themselves?

There are many different techniques and methods of generating work as an ensemble including improvisation, compositional tasks, scores, and writing, to name a few. There are also a range of historical and existing models, such as those introduced by leading 20th century pedagogs and artists, Grotowski, Lecoq, and Michael Chekhov, as well as techniques such as Viewpoints and Tectonic Theater Project's Moment Work. Underlying every approach to making new work, however, is a profound and intimate understanding, and the repeated and sustained practice of the act of collaboration itself.

A devised process is always new. It exists in relation with, and in reaction to, the other people in the room. Andy Horwitz, cultural producer, curator, critic, and Director of Programs at Skirball Cultural Center, quotes David Williams, former head of the MA in Devised Theatre at Dartington College of Arts in Devon, England, in his 2012 article, "The Politics of Cultural Production in Theater (Or Devise This!) Part I":

> All [the] work arises from particular personnel, contexts, and present concerns . . . materials arise out of the individuals making up a particular group. What are each person's particular abilities, facilities, fascinations, difficulties, etc.? In what ways can the performers themselves be enabled to "flare into appearance"? (Horwitz 2012)

This liveness—the chemistry of "these people, this place, this time" (Horwitz 2013)—is what makes this mode of creation the most challenging, and for those drawn to creating in this way, the most engaging.

But how does one teach something that is not codified or systematized and therefore repeatable? The answer is to engage with it directly in an experiential manner, not only as a process working towards production, but as a practice in and of itself. By placing students in the role of theatre maker with the goal of creating something original in an ensemble context with other theatre makers, they will encounter profound social, political, and phenomenological principles about the collaborative act, principles that are universally applicable beyond the rehearsal room, to any collaborative engagement.

The Politics of Collaboration

Those new to devising often expect the devising process to be equitable and democratic and that working in a group will mean working in agreement and without hierarchy. In practice however, there must be disagreement, conflicting views, and the challenging of ideas in order to make work that is interesting. This multiplicity of voices serves the work by offering ongoing and rigorous examination and exploration of ideas through the various eyes and creative minds of the ensemble. And there is in fact always hierarchy in some form present in the devising process, but working in a collaborative, process-oriented approach allows for the organizational structure in the rehearsal room to be fluid, adjusting in reaction to the work and the creative exploration rather than in a pre-existing, prescribed manner. "Actors, designers, writer(s) and director negotiate and consent to organizational hierarchies through process, not by default assignments of traditional assumptions" (Horwitz, 2013).

This can be a destabilizing, but ultimately liberating, discovery for those new to devising. Working like this demands that the ensemble member take on whatever role is required for the work at any given moment in the creative evolution of the piece. This might be, for example, the role of the "leader" creating vision, direction, and purpose for the group; the action-oriented "doer," running with and implementing the ideas the ensemble proposes; the "thinker," generating ideas and solving problems; the "challenger" playing devil's advocate, scrutinizing and evaluating: or the "listener," supporting and fostering cohesion in the group.

In an academic context, the mutability of roles within the ensemble gives room for students to explore the various sides of their individual personality and themselves as artists. In *The Moving Body*, Lecoq writes about the revelations students make while working in self-directed groups at the L'École Internationale de Théâtre Jacques Lecoq:

> ... students discover strengths as directors, authors, actors. The person who becomes powerful in the group is not necessarily the one who most wanted to take the lead: sometimes an unassuming personality reveals a powerful presence ... All such group dynamics emerge in the course of this type of work. (Lecoq 94)

Through a devising process, the actor will engage with the work from every angle and as the traditional duties in each discipline are blurred, she will learn to operate as a hybrid artist—an actor/creator.

The Practice of Collaboration

For sixty-one years, L'École Jacques Lecoq in Paris has been internationally recognized as the leading institution training artists in the collaborative creation of work with the explicit mission to produce a "young theatre of new work" (18). Lecoq stated that at his school:

> It is not just a matter of training actors, but of educating theatre artists of all kinds ... One of the school's unique features is to provide as broad and as durable a foundation as possible, since we know that each student will go on to make his own journey using the foundations we provide. (18)

At L'École Jacques Lecoq, over a third of the school day is dedicated to the students working together without the guidance of teachers. Working within the parameters of clearly defined assignments, these *auto-cours* (a direct translation is 'self-taught class') allow the students to experience unmediated and unguided collaboration and creation. Students are "thrown back on themselves and have to invent their own theatre" (23). It is through these *auto-cours* more than any other aspect of the Lecoq pedagogy that truly engenders the spirit of the performer/creator that is so central to the school's mission and most clearly reflects Lecoq's belief that "The greatest strength of the school is its students" (23).

Learning how to collectively conceive and create work cannot be taught theoretically, it can only be learned experientially. Regular repeated and varied opportunities for students to "get their hands dirty" and create work together are essential. These may include such things as different group sizes and group configurations, different duration of assignments, creation time, and of course, diverse and clearly defined creative prompts. Those facilitating the devising experience must avoid intervention in the groups' processes and resist shielding students from the challenges, frustrations, and disagreements inherent in any collaborative process. In return, students encounter conflicts, recognize recurring patterns of behavior in others, and in themselves, become versatile in navigating group dynamics, learn to negotiate and self-govern within fluid organizational hierarchies that arrive through the process, and most importantly, have the freedom to create.

The Philosophy of Collaboration

Creating work in a devised manner requires a seeming contradiction: total artistic investment in the work and simultaneous offering of the self to the work. In his article, "The Practice of Astonishment: Devising, Phenomenology and Jacques Lecoq," Jon Foley Sherman uses Rosalyn Diprose's term "radical giving" to shed light on the phenomenon that occurs within the collaborative act at the Lecoq school where "training seeks to instill commitment to being-given, not just to others, but also to *le jeu* and the shared work of creative discovery" (Sherman, Astonishment 161). *Le jeu* means 'game' and 'joy' and it refers to being at play and filled with the pleasure of performing. When the actor is truly playing or has *le jeu*, she is open, spontaneous, and truthfully present.

The devising process requires both giving and being-given to the process, to playing, to the group, to an idea, to the project, and to the promise of a successful outcome. Each member of the ensemble engages in a social and artistic contract to equally invest in the process and agree to a common goal. The members of the group share the risk and reap the rewards equally. With no pre-existing script and therefore no known outcome, the work will only be as good as the contributions of the ensemble members. In embarking on such a creative exploration, the ensemble must take a joint leap of faith that something worthy will emerge.

The performer/creator gives herself to the work by inhabiting a state of openness: the term used at the Lecoq school is a *disponibilité*. This is a physical and imaginative state of being ready, receptive, alert, and agile; willing to improvise off an idea, react and play with a fellow performer; embrace any "mistake" and turn it into possibility. But being *disponible* also involves a willingness to hear others' ideas. Anne Bogart has a wonderfully useful phrase; "hold tightly, let go lightly" (Bogart 161) that speaks to how the artist must deeply value and believe in every contribution they make toward the work and be willing to relinquish their hold on the contribution once it is offered up. As soon as an idea is shared, it is changed. It is heard and reinterpreted through different sets of ears, processed through multiple imaginations and becomes communal property for acceptance or rejection, suggestion, improvement, and inevitable alteration.

An essential guiding principle in devising is the question, "what does the story need?" By keeping this question as the primary filter through which all ideas and propositions are made and heard, the giving and giving up of ideas is no longer a personal or seemingly sacrificial act. It is no longer what the artist wants or needs, but what the work needs. This places the focus outside the individual and onto the story and in doing so, the work of art becomes bigger than the self.

Beyond the Rehearsal Room- Why Devise?

In the academic context, devising offers a training that goes beyond the paradigm of traditional theatre education. Where the majority of actor training programs in the U. S. focus on vocational tools and practical skills for production, and students are taught the modes of performance currently in vogue and commercially viable (Cynkutis 82), students who engage with a devised praxis learn modes of creation (Cynkutis). As Virginie Magnat states in her article "Devising Utopia," students who are given opportunities to make their own work collaboratively develop more than techniques; they build an artistic practice and learn "how to find inspiration from a variety of sources beyond the technical requirements of the acting profession" (Magnat) and they are empowered to discover their own "creative fulfillment irrespective of the market place" (Magnat 83).

From a broader educational perspective, working collectively embraces inter- and intra-disciplinary thinking, while offering alternative ways of negotiating power and giving voice within a group. Additionally, devising can be seen to challenge the central pedagogical tenets of higher education itself in that it upends the canonical Western privileging of the mind over body and reason over intuition and the experience of senses. Devising presents a process of creative expression that is fundamentally situated in the temporal and physical realities of the ensemble as it works together. "Writing on one's feet" and "thinking with the body" are phrases often used to describe the devising process in action. The individual body of the actor-creator and the collective body of the ensemble are the source and the site of the creative process in the act of devising. This primacy of the individual and collective bodies makes devising an act of embodied creativity.

Conclusion

The process of making work in a devised manner demands a profound generosity toward others and to something greater than oneself—that is the workings of the ensemble, the creative journey, and the story being collectively told. Devising demands a rigorously open state and a sustained level of "extraordinary listening" (Bogart 32) and a willingness to be adaptive to the process: to adopt and shed roles and traverse disciplines. Working in this manner requires a unique kind of human communication, an ethos of giving and being given to creativity. In this light, devising has profound transformative potential beyond the rehearsal room. It offers a model of engagement that has the power to affect the culture at large and change how people listen, think, and work together.

AFTERWORD

The concept of team roles is taken primarily from the work of two thinkers: Peter Honey and Meredith Belbin, with contributions from Michael Brown, Director of the MFA European Devised Performance Practice at Columbia College as shared with me during the Network of Ensemble Theater Conference, Chicago, May 2016.

Works Cited

Bogart, Anne and Tina Landau. *The Viewpoints Book: A Practical Guide to Viewpoints and Composition*. New York: Theatre Communications Group, 2005. Print.

Collins, J., Groff, R., Dyer, E., Kaufman, M., Miller, W. "What is Devised Theatre? A Round Table Discussion." *The Dramatist*, vol. 17. Mar/April 2015.

Horwitz, Andy. "The Politics of Cultural Production In Theater (Or, Devise This!), Part I." *Culturebot*, 30 Nov. 2012. Web. <http://www.culturebot.org/2012/11/15219/the-politics-of-cultural-production-in-theater-or-devise-this-part>.

Horwitz, Andy. "The Politics of Cultural Production In Theater (Or, Devise This!), Part III." *Culturebot*, 13 Feb. 2013. Web. <http://www.culturebot.org/2013/02/15952/the-politics-of-cultural-production-in-theater-or-devise-this-part-iii/>.

Kaplan, Shirley, former Director of the Theatre Program, Sarah Lawrence College, personal email, September 2017.

Lecoq, Jacques. *The Moving Body (Le Corps Poétique): Teaching Creative Theatre*. Trans. David Bradby. London: Methuen, 2001. Print.

Magnat, Virginie, "Devising Utopia, or Asking for the Moon." *Theatre Topics*, vol. 15, no. 1, March 2005. Print.

Novick, Rebecca, "Please, Don't Start a Theater Company! Next-Generation Arts Institutions and Alternative Career Paths." *GIA Reader*, vol. 22, no. 1, Spring 2011. Web. <http://www.giarts.org/article/please-dont-start-theater-company>.

Rinear, Sheila. "Kirk Lynn & Rude Mechanicals." *The Dramatist*, Mar. / Apr. 2015. Print.

Sarah Lawrence College. BFA Degree in Theatre. Undergraduate Academics Catalogue. Feb. 2017. Web. <http://www.sarahlawrence.edu/undergraduate/arts/theatre/>.

Sherman, Jon Foley. "The Practice of Astonishment: Devising, Phenomenology, and Jacques Lecoq." *Theatre Topics*, vol. 20, no. 2, Sept. 2010, pp. 95, Johns Hopkins UP. Print.

Theater of the Vulnerable:
How Being a Blue Man for Twelve Years Taught Me about Acting, Directing, and Teaching

By Isaac Eddy

I have always had stage fright, since the fourth grade when we performed *A Midsummer Night's Dream, the Musical*. I was playing Puck. I had my shirt off. I was wearing these green shorts that my mom made me. She stapled cloth leaves on my cut-offs to make them resemble what a wood nymph might wear. I was supposed to start my solo, "Lord, what fools these mortals be," but all I could think of was that the whole school was looking at me, and that these staples were scratching my legs. For just a moment, I blacked out. I completely forgot what I was supposed to sing. I came to my senses and, awkwardly, finished the song. This early experience planted a seed: a fear of messing up, looking stupid, and failing. Even so, there was something that kept on drawing me to live performance. In many ways, continuing to follow a career path in something that I was afraid of has informed who I am more than anything else in my life. This began a life-long discovery of the power that vulnerability holds in the performing arts.

So much of our lives is lived online now; a world where we have exposure but are not truly exposed. Our digital selves on social media don't need to face fear because we choose, meticulously, how to present ourselves and where to engage. This world lures us with the promise of the mouse click and screen tap: complete power and control. It seems that vulnerability, in many ways, is on the verge of extinction. But theater, live performance, has the ability to enliven the vulnerable in all of us. In theater, there is an unspoken contract between those of us on and behind the stage and the audience: In this house we will share our rough and incomplete edges; together we will strive to solve the unsolvable; we will analyze and unpack the unjust and idiosyncratic elements of the human condition.

Shortly after college I moved to Los Angeles to work in film. Missing live performance drew me to discover footage of the show *Blue Man Group*. Although the Blue Men on stage don't speak, a lot is said during the show with drums, artwork, and with their eyes. There was a humor and a sensitivity to the Blue Man character that I immediately understood. I drove to an open call in Las Vegas the next week and was told I needed to be a better drummer. So I went back to Los Angeles, hired a drum teacher, practiced four hours a day for six months, auditioned again, and I got the gig. I was lucky enough to perform the show full-time for twelve and a half years in Chicago, Las Vegas, London, and New York City. It's been two years since I left the show to teach theater at Johnson State College in Vermont. It's taken my departure from *Blue Man Group* to see how much that character has changed how I look at acting, directing, and theater in general. It's there where my real journey with vulnerability really began.

There is a moment in Constantin Stanislavski's system of acting that is referenced as transformation (Stanislavski 299). This is when a new self is formed that is a combination of the actor and the character he or she is portraying. Transformation is achieved when the actor's

Photo by NYC Department of Environmental Protection

goals fall perfectly in sync with the character's goals. I think that one of the reasons the Blue Man is so compelling is because these goals are intrinsically in sync throughout the whole show. It is the actor who has to catch all those marshmallows in his mouth; and it's also the Blue Man. It is the actor who needs desperately to assess the attention of the audience and to try and bring them together; this is also the Blue Man's need. It's the actor who is focused completely on being physically aware of the other two Blue Men on stage; this is also the Blue Man's ultimate focus and intent. I've performed the show roughly four thousand times. That's almost eight months straight, 24 hours a day of being on stage in front of an audience in bald and blue makeup. I don't think Stanislavski meant for his transformation to be taken to that extreme. Often, when talking about performing in a long running show, it's the boredom and the grind that is discussed. "How do you keep it fresh?" was a common question when I told people the length of time I performed in the *Blue Man Group*. But the way we are trained as Blue Men and the super-objectives of the character make it so that if you stay on target as an actor, each show is genuinely its own challenge and continually "fresh." The show incorporates the audience so much that they are considered a fourth character. From the rise of our welding masks at the top of the show, it is immediately apparent that each audience takes on a different tenor and vibe which can completely change the purpose of each scene. To a rowdy audience, the opening scenes can make us seem like we are scientists trying to tame a wild beast so that we can study it. If the audience is quiet, sleepy, or distracted, the Blue Man can appear to be more of a spiritual leader looking to create a gestalt experience.

Performing as a Blue Man so many times gave me the opportunity to explore every potential interpretation of every single beat in the show. It was a rare and valuable assignment for an actor: inhabit this character for a large chunk of your adult life, turn it inside out, experiment with new interpretations, make mistakes and try again a different way the next night, and (perhaps most telling of all) watch

Issac (left) performing at a Hurricane Irene "I Vermont NY" benefit, with Amanda Palmer (center). *Photo by Robert Eddy*

the character evolve as you, yourself, grow and change. A prominent reason the interpretation of the Blue Man character is so malleable is because he does not speak. Since leaving the show, I found that this constriction of being mute on stage, which is counter-intuitively completely freeing, can be applied as a learning tool to all characters and to many styles of acting. The character has taught me four main lessons that I use every day in my current role as a director and as a teacher.

Lesson One: Listening

The first lesson is listening. A lot can be learned about the people around you and about yourself when you just . . . shut up for a little bit. Often a solution isn't needed immediately. It's more powerful to just actively listen. This is true for learning more about the people and the world around you but it's also true for yourself and your own body.

Jerzy Grotowski calls this process the Via Negativa. To properly learn how to perform with any true authenticity, we must first

Theater of the Vulnerable

take away (Grotowski 16). Via Negativa is a process of unlearning rather than filling your head with new information. The point is to attempt to remove the wall between desire and action in the actor. There are blockages within ourselves that disrupt the communication of our inner and external selves. The non-speaking Blue Man forced me to listen to my body, and to allow myself to allow gesture to precede thought. When I was training for the show in the East Village rehearsal space in New York City, I developed a nerve pain that was very disconcerting. Each time I practiced drumming or any of the other physical elements of the show, a nerve near my left shoulder would freeze up so badly that a swath of my skin from my pinky through my arm and neck to my left cheek would go numb. Sometimes the numbing would be so debilitating that I couldn't even control a small bit of drool from coming out of the left side of my mouth. I feared that this was a sign that I wasn't built for the physical demands of the show. I was training for my dream gig and it was possible that I wouldn't make the cut simply because I didn't have enough stamina and endurance. The possibility of this was heartbreaking. I was watching the show for training almost every night at the time, and it was there that I had my own Via Negativa revelation. I was sitting in the audience letting my mind wander, waiting for the show to begin. When the pre-show music finally bumped up in volume and the lights dimmed indicating the show's commencement, my nerve pain immediately kicked in. For the first time I realized that what I thought was a physical problem was completely psychological. This could, in fact, be traced back to my stage fright spurred by my failed performance as a singing Puck. My mind, albeit trying to be helpful, was placing a giant blockage of fear between me and this role I so eagerly wanted to play. When I realized that it was a psychological problem and not a physical one, I was able to tackle it through gesture, not mental exercise or analysis. Simple repetition of the character's posture, his walk, and his frame's shape in space was what allowed me to work through the nerve pain. This gestural repetition slowly worked away at the psychological blocks that I had unknowingly placed in my way. I learned how to listen to my body in a new way because of this nerve problem. And the result was a new level of trust that my body can generously give me new information about a character's perspective. I could only receive this information when I unlearned enough to listen.

Lesson Two: Innocence does not equal stupid

A large part of the Blue Man character is looking at the world anew. When playing the role I didn't make judgments on what I saw. I took everything in with equal value because it all might hold the key to connection. So much can be communicated to an audience simply by standing with minimal movement and looking back at them. This openness is silent but it still speaks. There is an element of danger. There is also a savant focus. There is a tenderness or a love that is exchanged at this moment as well. The one thing that this innocence does not embody is stupidity. This was a revelation to me. When I was younger I was always afraid to speak up when I didn't understand something. I felt it was relinquishing what small bit of social control I had. The Blue Man character allowed me to feel empowered in this state of innocence, and showed me how much I could truly learn when I was open for it.

At the end of the school year, *Blue Man Group* plays many matinee shows primarily for school groups. The energy of these shows can sometimes be difficult to navigate because it can feel like the teenagers are excited but not willing to go on the show's journey with us. If these shows are approached incorrectly they can devolve into an hour and a half of teenage yells, screams, and taunts. When we enter the audience half way through the show there can be a throng of arms pulling at us trying to get our attention. The goal of the show, creating a community with the audience, can easily be lost when this happens. But, as is the case in most facets of life, some of my most memorable and moving moments as a Blue Man have been during these unfocused and noisy shows. There was one teenage boy who was especially loud and eager for me to approach him. Often if an audience member is too brazen with the character and tries to talk to the actor under the makeup I often ignore them. This is mainly because it can take me out of character but it also has the potential to dismantle the performative contract I've created with others in the audience. But there was something about this boy's energy at this particular show that my Blue Man was interested in. I moved closer to him, walking on the audience's chair backs, dipping my head low to get a better look. As I approached, he yelled louder and waved his arms more excitedly for me to come closer. His friends laughed and pushed him, calling for others to look at what was happening. I could have interpreted this as a sad "birthday clown" moment. Maybe I was simply being laughed at by a bunch of teenagers but instead I chose to take in all the information with an innocent curiosity. I jumped off the chairs and got very, very close to his face. The drummer and the rest of the band in the loft were watching my every move and the music got more frenetic the closer my face got to his. This could have been an act of aggression but my eyes were open wide and there was almost a smile on my face. Instead of trying to tamp down this teenage energy, I was taking it all in with all of my senses. The boy didn't push me, or make faces, or yell to try and make me flinch. Instead, I had an intimate close-up view of this stranger's face slowly soften from a fidgety and unfocused excitement to a calm resolve. His group of friends around him became still and contemplative as well. This was just a fleeting moment but it was wonderful to witness from such close range, and it was achieved by simply utilizing innocence and wonder.

 Neuroscientists have proven that experiencing awe expands our mental capacity and makes us more empathic and loving (Piff 885). We can't get to awe without confronting the unknown and we can't get there with Wikipedia alone. A friend of mine who is a mathematician told me once that he is in the business of being confused. When he is not in a state of confusion that means the problem is solved and he's no longer being a good mathematician. He sees his job as continually seeking out that confusion. The same is true in dynamic and engaging theater: seek confusion, confront the darkness with wide eyes, and put the awe back in "awesome."

As Blue Men, we often talk after the show about how some audiences can send mixed messages about their impressions of the show. Since a major element of the performance is us peering out into the audience trying to see what they think and feel, one would think that we would know immediately what is working and what isn't. But we, like any performers, can be wrong about this perception. There is a specific type of Blue Man show where the audience response is low and lethargic. As an actor it can feel like this low energy can feed on itself and slowly steer the entire show into the ground. The drumsticks feel heavier and less responsive, like they're made of lead; my body takes longer to respond, like it's a bag of sand; and the audience would act like they were preparing for some sort apathetic mutiny by choosing their phone's screen over our high-octane performance. After the show we get a quick drink of water and a makeup check in the mirror before we go to the lobby for one final moment with the audience as they file out of the house. More than once we have exchanged comments backstage about how hard the show was only to receive the most heartfelt, personal, and moving praise from audience members in the lobby. Cheering and applause is not always the best indicator of success, and silence, obviously, does not always mean failure. If you stand truly open to receive whatever may come in live performance, the results can be very surprising and uplifting.

Lesson Three: Contradiction is Good

In his seminal book, *To the Actor*, Michael Chekhov writes about simultaneous multiple selves as "three different beings," each with his or her own function and independence:

> While incorporating your character on the stage you use your emotions, voice and your mobile body. These constitute the "building material" from which the higher self, the real artist in you, creates a character for the stage. The higher self simply takes possession of that building material. As soon as this

happens, you begin to feel that you are standing apart from, or rather above, the material and, consequently, above your everyday self. That is because you now identify yourself with that creative, higher "I" which has become active. You are now aware of both your expanded self and your usual, everyday "I" existing within you simultaneously, side by side. While creating you are two selves, and you are able to distinguish clearly between the different functions they fulfill (Chekhov 87).

Chekhov continues with this image, explaining that the higher self represents inspiration which has a tendency to overpower the other selves. The "artist" higher self needs the everyday self to restrict it and convert inspiration to expression. According to Chekhov, we can think of the everyday self as controlling the canvas on which our higher consciousness paints. Without the framing and restriction of the canvas there is no place for the paint to go and all referential meaning can be lost. Once this interaction between the artist self and the everyday self is achieved it makes way for the third level of consciousness, "the Character created by yourself" (89).

The higher consciousness, needing the everyday self to restrict it and give a frame for expression, resonates with my process of discovering my Blue Man character. I like to think of the Chekhovian "sweet spot" for an enlightened performance as the center of a Venn diagram where all of these three selves overlap. It took me a year of performing the Blue Man full time at the Luxor in Las Vegas before I could feel myself entering into the center of those three circles. It took a lengthy time to achieve this because that's how long I needed for the building blocks of my everyday self, my higher self, and my "character created by myself" to grow enough to overlap with one another and truly co-exist. I distinctly remember the moment on stage when this happened. We were seated at the "feast" table with a newly minted fourth member of our tribe whom we had just plucked from the audience. The purpose of this scene is to get a closer look at a single audience member to see if we can delineate and create any new forms of connection with the audience as a whole. We, the Blue Men, slowly set the table for a meal of some sort. But with each object we reveal, we see if we can glean any information from our new guest on stage as to the true meaning behind these foreign objects. There is a lot to continually process and re-process in this scene: this new being on stage with us ("Are they dangerous?"), their reaction to the objects on the feast table ("Are we doing everything correctly?"), and the audience as a whole ("Is this gesture helping or hurting our relationship?"). The answers to these questions are constantly changing since the response depends on rapid-fire check-ins between object, guest, audience, and the other two Blue Men.

In the first year of performing, it was close to impossible to take in and exchange any real information at these check-ins. I was too worried that I would miss a cue or an important piece of information if I allowed myself to focus so much on each moment or beat. The result, of course, was a performance in which I was only half present. But finally, at the feast table during one particular show, I allowed myself for the first time to forget all of the direction that I had been receiving through training and my first year performing. I trusted my body to properly guide me through all the necessary beats of the scene which made space for my higher self to take in all of this real-time information and allow it to truly affect me, physically and emotionally. The most exciting part of this moment was that I was taking in this information simultaneously as myself and as my character. I like to think of this moment as the point in time where my Blue Man was born.

The Blue Man character is an innocent, but he is also a bomb squad super hero. He is an ancient shaman, but he is also a mad scientist of the future. He is a team player, but he is also a punk rock trickster. The training I had in acting did not prepare me to play a character with so many simultaneous contradictions. In the first year of performing there was always one side of these opposites that I couldn't portray. It didn't feel "real" to me to inhabit both of them at the same time. Real or not real, I began to force myself to engage with the audience and the other Blue Men from all points of this spectrum. It felt uncomfortable at first, less of a clean and polished performance and more like I was showing my partners on stage my dirty laundry. But after a while, something very interesting happened. I realized that this liminal space between all these opposites, this rough performance where I could vacillate between two seemingly incompatible motivations, was more human, more real, than anything. I always thought of contradiction as weak and ill-planned. But if we are comfortable enough to stay in this liminal space for a moment there is a strength and a true depth there. The Blue Man taught me the meaning of Walt Whitman's famous words: "Do I contradict myself? Very well, then I contradict myself. I am large, I contain multitudes" (Whitman 67).

Lesson Four: Performance is Transgressive

Blue Man taught me my fourth life lesson of performance when I attended graduate school at Brooklyn College and studied performance and interactive media art. By this point, I had been with the show for nine years. I was performing full time and cast as captain at Blue Man's original venue, the Astor Place Theatre in the East Village, and biking down to my MFA classes during the day. It quickly became a wonderful daily mashup of theory and practice. I was reading and discussing critical theories of performance during the day and then looking at how it applied to my own Blue Man performances at night. Suddenly, I was rethinking these moments I'd experienced a thousand times with the audience in new ways by utilizing the theoretical frameworks of Bertolt Brecht, Antonin Artaud, Michel Foucault, Jacques Rancière, Peggy Phelan, and Philip Auslander. This was where I had my fourth and final revelation on performance and vulnerability: Performance is transgressive.

Peggy Phelan writes that performance "becomes itself through disappearance" (Phelan 146), meaning that the core essence of live performance is that it is non-reproducible. This experience cannot be repeated. It is fleeting ephemera meant only for the people in the room, here and now. Since it can't be duplicated it goes against the main tenet of capitalism making it inherently transgressive. Phelan continues, "Performance clogs the smooth machinery of reproductive representation necessary to the circulation of capital" (148). This is one of the few exchanges we have in our society that is not completely commodified. Sure, people pay to see theater, and yes, live performances are reproduced and commodified all the time. But even so, I believe that Phelan has touched on the answer to this core question: In a world where we have lifetimes of cathartic entertainment continually streamable on the smartphone in our pocket, why does theater even exist anymore?

"Why theatre?" is the question that all performance theorists have had to answer once film, television, and then the internet were created, replacing theater as the new forms of performative storytelling. Bertolt Brecht wanted us to leave the suspension of disbelief to the moviegoers. He aimed for his audiences to be vitally aware of all of the elements of the live performance happening in front of them, to create a dissonance in the audience that might incite social change (Brecht 144).

Jerzy Grotowski, who was plainly aware of the transgressive nature of live performance, said that theater was meant to be "poor." His term, "poor theatre," is in reference to the abandonment of the material glitz of costumes, sets, sound, and lighting to exploit the one thing that theater has that film and television doesn't: a live-wire interactive connection between the audience and the performer (19). Ann Bogart says that one of the greatest achievements in theater is when it is embarrassing. What she means is that live performance is one of the few places left in our culture in which vulnerability is currency and not a weakness (Bogart 115).

Reading and discussing these theories with my colleagues at Brooklyn College and then biking into Manhattan to perform the Blue Man show was the first time I was made aware of this contract that the performers on stage have with their audience. Every night, our simple presence in the theater is a silent agreement that we

Theater of the Vulnerable

will engage in the thrilling and terrifying exploration of the human condition. What makes theater unique is that we do this exploration together. The very framework of this delicate exchange is cause for the vulnerability that is so rare in our contemporary social systems. This is why theater still exists. This is why it's as important now as it ever has been, smartphones be damned. This contract still has the ability to change the world—and it still does.

While focusing on this vulnerable exchange between the performer and the audience, I discovered that it exists in teaching as well. To put it in performative terms, teaching seemed like the ultimate immersive theater experience. Teacher vs. student was a relationship where the stakes were potentially much higher than that of performer and audience, and the exchange bumps up as well to a new level of interactivity. In the classroom the act is not finished when the teacher stops talking. The act is finished when the student shows what she has learned. This was exciting for me. I quickly learned that I received the same type of performance energy and adrenaline when I was devising courses and teaching as I did when I was acting on stage. Since this relationship seemed so familiar, I was eager to see if the lessons I learned on stage as a Blue Man could be applied to teaching and directing. Before my Blue Man turned into a teenager, thirteen years with the show, I moved my family and our chickens from Brooklyn back to my home state of Vermont to teach at Johnson State College.

When reflecting on my first lesson learned as a Blue Man, listening, I often think of Frank Hauser and Russell Reich's book, *Notes on Directing*:

> Please, PLEASE be decisive. As the director, you have three weapons: "Yes," "No," and "I don't know." Use them. Don't dither; you can always change your mind later. Nobody minds that. What they do mind is the two-minute agonizing when all the actor has asked is, "Do I get up now?" (45)

I use this strong advice all the time when directing and teaching. When I directed my first production at Johnson State College I learned a fourth weapon: "What do you think?" There is most certainly the problem with "dithering," as Hauser and Reich call it, when you invite this type of discussion in the middle of rehearsal, but I've found that the returns can be worth it especially with student ensembles. I learned in *Blue Man Group* and in long form improv comedy that the whole of the ensemble is smarter than the sum of its parts when given the right communication tools. This hive-mind can only be achieved through listening and through the director setting up a rehearsal structure in which this creative engagement is encouraged. I chose Sarah Ruhl's *Eurydice* as my directorial debut at the college, primarily due to the expressionistic, open-ended, and frankly impossible nature of the set and stage directions. I wanted these problems to be tackled not only by the designers (primarily students), but by the acting ensemble as well. I continually asked the ensemble what they thought, not as a directorial choice but because I really wanted to know. Their ideas might be better than mine. The hierarchy of director or teacher over actor or student evened out when I listened to their ideas about these key moments in the show. The ensemble's comprehension of the play's complex themes deepened as they tackled these problems with me, and so did their performances. The end result was an innovative and exciting piece that I only had a part in creating.

We built a catwalk stage where the two halves of the audience faced in on themselves, becoming a part of the set and the sight lines. For many parts of the show multi-camera live videos were projected onto the back wall of the theater. By presenting key scenes from simultaneous multiple angles, the audience had to actively choose whether they were going to watch the projection on the screen or the actors right in front of them. I felt that this engaged the audience in an exciting way with one of the central themes of *Eurydice*: the plasticity of memory and identity. In scene ten at the pivotal moment where Orpheus looks back at Eurydice thus sealing her doomed fate,

Ruhl gives one of her wonderfully impossible stage directions: "He turns towards her, startled. Orpheus looks at Eurydice. Eurydice looks at Orpheus. The world falls away" (Ruhl 60).

The "world falling away" in our production meant the instant breakdown of the theatrical façade. The stage inverted from the dark underworld to the bright work lights, revealing all the dusty corners of the theater itself. The hum and pings and drops of water that made up the layered soundscape were abruptly cut at this moment as well. We were left with a deafening silence as Orpheus and Eurydice stand facing each other in this harsh unromantic light. This I knew could translate easily but . . . what happens next? Orpheus and Eurydice plead with one another and try desperately to salvage their bond, but they speak simultaneously and cannot take in what the other is saying. This breakdown of communication is an emotional reveal to the viewer of how flawed their love is, how flawed all love can be. We may have found a way to represent the world falling away but where do we go from there? What about this gaping distance between these two characters? How can we show that, even though they are standing so close together at this moment? Instead of setting this aside to solve with the designers, I put it to the actors. Time was tight and we had much more to work through but even so, I knew there was an exciting puzzle piece here and I needed help finding it.

We projected their faces in close-up on the back wall and that projection loomed large over the two actors standing center stage. They started making faces at one another and walking around the stage catching glimpses of different angles of their own large, projected heads. They were half in character making jokes with one another about how they looked on the screen. As they moved, there was a moment that we all saw and immediately knew was the answer to our way back in. The two actors were standing about 15 feet from one another facing each other center stage. One was so far upstage and the other so far downstage that they could not look at each other at all. But the high depth of field camera mashed the distance between them so on the screen it looked as if they were gazing into

Eurydice at Johnson State College. 2016. *Photo by Robert Eddy*

each other's eyes about to kiss. It was the perfect visual representation of the scene's emotional distancing and it was discovered by listening to the ensemble and allowing them to play.

A second example of my lessons from *Blue Man Group* informing my pedagogy is from the same play but with a different actor. The student who played the role of Father in *Eurydice* is one of the strongest actors we had in the program, but he still held tightly to crutches that I find common with young actors. Early in the rehearsal process I could see that he was locking into specific gestures and speech rhythm with each of his scenes. He began to repeat them when we would revisit the scenes the next day. If a character comes easily to an actor I am not prone to shoehorn layers of complexity and difficulty just for the sake of it, although I did find that his refining of the Father's perspective and objectives so early in the process had the potential of stultifying this wonderful character even before he had the chance to take his first breath. I find that there is a trend among young actors to focus heavily on looking natural and honest, so much so that they lose sight of the most important part of acting.

They are communicating with other characters and they don't know how they are being received without active listening. Without this vulnerable connection between actor and actor, all the other work is lost. I could see that this student playing the father was so intent on getting it right that he wasn't allowing himself to explore this unknown with his relationship to Eurydice. I saw myself in him when I was wrestling with the contradictions in the Blue Man character my first year with the show. But I also saw myself now as the director potentially attempting to yet again side-step the coexistence of multiple selves. I was not entirely sure how to push this student back from a clean and consistent performance into the uncomfortable world of listening and discovery. In the end, the result came through the repetition of unspoken gesture that was not devised by me but by the playwright herself.

In scene three the Father attempts to make the underworld more familiar to his daughter. "The father creates a room out of string for Eurydice. He makes four walls and a door out of string. Time passes. It takes time to build a room out of string" (Ruhl 34). String is referenced throughout the play with allusions to memory and our interconnectedness, but its use in this scene has other connotations as well. The Father is building the flimsy visual idea of a home, not an actual home. This shows the delicate and complicated relationship between a parent and child who is not a child anymore. The Father's role is no longer to provide tangible sustenance for his daughter, but instead to provide space for her to discover and rediscover who she is. The power of this message is in the mandate by Ruhl that the audience witnesses the physical creation of this room and that it "takes time." It was the building of this room out of string where I saw this student enter into that murky coexistence of the everyday self, the higher self, and the character, and it informed the rest of his performance.

The first few times the actor made the room he was rushing. Not wanting to take up too much time and trying to push on to the next moment where he could finally talk again made him fumble

Eurydice at Johnson State College. 2016. *Photo by Robert Eddy*

and make mistakes with the build so that, inevitably, he'd have to start over again. I pulled him aside and I reminded him that this was supposed to take time, the playwright said so herself, and that it was fascinating to watch. I told him to just simply focus on the task and trust that we are interested. The blockage of trying to nail a "perfect" performance slowly left his posture as his eyes focused simply on the ball of string in his hands. All that was left was an objective that was identical to the character of the Father and to this actor who was standing in front of an audience, poised for the unknown.

    I know it's much easier to encourage people to engage in vulnerability than it is to actually get up and do it. This is especially true when the direction is coming from me who happens to have a volume of privilege where vulnerability could arguably come much easier. I'm white, male, heterosexual, cisgender, and able-bodied. We've heard a lot from that intersectional perspective over the last few thousand years. Vulnerability comes in many forms, forms that I don't even know about. But I want to know about them, and the world should know about them as well, so to that I say . . . I'm listening.

Works Cited

Bogart, Anne. *A Director Prepares: Seven Essays on Art and Theatre*. London: Routledge, 2010. Print.

Brecht, Bertolt. *Brecht on Theatre: The Development of an Aesthetic*. New York: Hill & Wang, 1992. Print.

Chekhov, Michael. *To the Actor*. New York: Routledge, 2002. Print.

Grotowski, Jerzy. *Towards a Poor Theatre*. New York: Routledge, 2002. Print.

Hauser, Frank, and Russell Reich. *Notes on Directing: 130 Lessons in Leadership from the Director's Chair*. London: Walker, 2003. Print.

Phelan, Peggy. *Unmarked: The Politics of Performance*. London: Routledge, 2006. Print.

Piff, Paul K., et al. "Awe, the Small Self, and Prosocial Behavior." *Journal of Personality and Social Psychology*, vol. 108, no.6, 2015, pp. 883-99. Print.

Ruhl, Sarah. *Eurydice*. London: Methuen Drama, 2010. Print.

Stanislavsky, Constantin, and Elizabeth Reynolds Hapgood. *An Actor Prepares*. New York: Routledge, 1989. Print.

Whitman, Walt. *Leaves of Grass: The Original*. 1855. Print.

Neil LaBute and Cosmin Chivu on stage at the Schimmel Center.
Photo by Scott Wynn

An Interview with Neil Labute:
Part of the Master Series at the Pace School of the Performing Arts, Schimmel Center for the Arts, New York City

By Cosmin Chivu

Cosmin: Welcome to Pace. Hello everyone, it's good to see you all. I want to point out that Neil doesn't live in New York, but is currently in New York for a very particular reason. Could you tell us about that?

Neil: I'm working on a play at a place called MCC (founded in 1986 as Manhattan Class Company], in the West Village at the Lucille Lortel and I've worked with them for the last ten years or so. I've worked with them on seven shows or something like that and this is the first sequel they've done for anything. I did a play called *Reasons to Be Pretty* a few years ago, and so I wrote a play called *Reasons to be Happy* and we came up with relatively few. So we're in rehearsals now, halfway through rehearsals, I guess, and we will start previews in the middle of May, and that's why I'm here because I'm also directing.

Cosmin: Is it an open run?

Neil: No, it's a subscription theater so it's their regular kind of six-week run, with some room for extension, but we're pretty limited.

Cosmin: How many projects have you directed, plays that you wrote, in New York?

Neil: Fewer in New York than other places. I've directed probably more in London or in L. A. I've only done two or three, maybe four here. It's deceptive because I've done a couple benefits for MCC which were plays and sometimes collections of scenes so it's been a couple of different things actually. But in terms of plays: I did a show called *The Mercy Seat* a few years ago, and then I did a play called *Wrecks* that we started in Europe and then brought over here, and then this one. I wasn't supposed to be here for this one. This was supposed to happen next year, but they had a play fall out of their season and we moved this into the slot because I was supposed to be directing for an LA adaptation of *Miss Julie*, which is still going on. I'm just not directing it, or I'm late for rehearsal.

Cosmin: Your adaptation of *Miss Julie*?

Neil: Yeah. I took a translation in the public domain, and then took the play, as you do when you adapt a Swedish play that was written in the 1880s. Sometimes you adapt it and keep it set exactly where it is. I took the setting and changed it to Long Island, in a quick easy way to say it's kind of like a *Great Gatsby*-ish *Miss Julie* that takes place in 1929 in a beautiful estate on Long Island. It's been moved from its time but I think all of the thematic stuff is still in place.

Photo by Scott Wynn

Cosmin: What inspired your commitment to theater in the first place? And how long ago was that?

Neil: It's hard to remember a time when I didn't like theater, but it's hard to trace back equally what it was. I didn't grow up in a family of . . . you know, sitting around the piano singing show tunes. I grew up in a very blue-collar working class family in Washington

Photo by Scott Wynn

of South America. So you are very much perceived as an American writer. How do you see that transition from American writer and why do you think Europe likes and wants your work?

Neil: You're never sure why. Hopefully it's a good story that people are latching on to—the story, and characters, and they feel that whatever language it's in that it's worth telling. I've also gotten a lot of work done in Germany. I think it's just that heritage of Western theater. Some people want to remove the text from the equation and others are very much embracing the idea that a good play is a good play. And some of them are fantastic, and I've seen productions where I couldn't recognize my play. I mean in the sense that I don't speak the language, but also on top of that the set is something that . . . I can remember a scene where there's an office and yet there's sand on the floor, a cactus in the corner cause that's American, I guess. It's like I have no idea what scene this is, and it's my play but that's their vision of America and this play. And you kind of have to roll with those things. I'm not one to go and stop this production. I know writers that have done that kind of thing. But for me it's just sort of the enjoyment of having that story be told and reimagined by somebody else. So I've been lucky. I think popularity goes in waves. I think at the heart of it there's a good story there. I feel like I'm a storyteller. Whether I'm writing about relationships or I'm writing about families, you're ultimately trying to say that this is something universal. Even if you've never had that experience or know what it's like to work in an American warehouse or be in a business. But people know what it's like to have friends or to cheat on people or fall in love or fall out of love, and so at the heart of that, they see a story that's going to make sense to them.

Cosmin: What inspires you in general? What makes you go "Oh, I want to write a play about that"?

Neil: That comes from so many different places. It's usually not theme. I don't sit around and think, "Oh well, I must write about gun control." I actually wrote a play about gun control, but that wasn't my idea, somebody came up to me and asked if I could write a short play about gun control. It's about a man who's lost his wife and he's resorting to increasingly frightening tactics to get her back. And that's what it was to me. It's not really about gun control. But I don't sit around and think "Oh, racism is important to write about." I'm not a political writer really, you know. Human politics I'm interested in but not really the two-party system or those kind of things. Sometimes it's just a story or just an idea and what if I put these two people together, it comes in fractured ways. Sometimes it's a line of dialogue. But rarely is it the same thing. And you just kind of know it when you hear it in your head. I try and, not that I dislike writing, I love writing, but I want to do it only when I'm moved to do it. I write all the time in my head, my mind never turns off but that's all part of the process. So once I'm in a piece, and I know that that's what I want to do, the rest of life becomes increasingly less interesting. I'm going to sit down and write. Writing will just kind of take over because I can't get away from the story. They kind of track me down as much as I track them down. You know, we kind of meet in a dark alley and yeah, it's sort of a weird homosexual event. And we exchange numbers, and somebody calls. I don't always know where the story is going to go, I don't spend time plotting every second of it. And some critics will say "Yeah I can tell." But when it's best, I think it's because it has revealed itself in a mysterious way to me, and ultimately that extends to an audience, that they watch it and go, "I have no idea where this is going." Moment to moment, it feels a bit more like life. People don't always get what's coming to them. There's not always a happy ending. And so when you go to the movies or a play, and the ending is happy, the audience may feel slighted. You can't tell everything in ninety minutes, that's just how stories are.

Cosmin: I want to get a little more specific. I'm going to name some of the plays that you wrote, non-chronological order because I don't necessarily think that's very important. I want to know what's behind the stories that you're portraying, if there's any truth or anything that inspired you from real life and I'm going to start with *Reasons To Be Pretty*. What was the process?

Neil: *Reasons To Be Pretty* actually came from the idea that—I guess there were two things. At the time I wrote it, I had already written *The Shape of Things* and *Fat Pig* and decided that I'm going to write another play. The first two plays had the same structure, they each had the same number of characters, two men, two women, and one man had made this emotional journey through both of them. So I'm going to do that again. They both were extensively about physical beauty and the way we deal with beauty or what is beautiful or how we want to change. There's something about the physicality of our looks. And I had the notion or the idea of what would happen if somebody said to their partner or their partner hear[d] that they were not thought to be the most attractive person around. But they like them, they love them, they want to be with them, but beauty wasn't that important to them. And I wondered how that felt, gender-wise. And I started randomly asking people, I asked both men and women, and most of the guys were like, "Yeah, I mean, you know, that would be… but we're going to stay together? Yeah. That's alright." And it's like you want to be attracted to your partner. But it was a deal breaker for the women that I talked to. "If it's not even that important in the guy, but if he does not find me attractive, then we're done." And so I thought that was interesting. And so that was the catalyst for that story. But ultimately, it's not just about that. I hope it's about relationships and crisis and you could've thrown anything, a match, onto that relationship and it would've sparked to ignite in a way for them to head in opposite directions. So while I wanted it to fit into that mold of that idea of beauty, it ultimately wasn't about, you know, he loved the way this girl was and looked and he just said something in relation to another girl that she was just regular-looking. And then the struggle was to try and get her back. Ultimately to find out that he shouldn't get back with her because it's better to let her go. So that's how that came about.

Neil LaBute with Cosmin Chivu. *Photo by Scott Wynn*

Cosmin: Let's talk about *The Shape of Things*. Did the structure come to you right away? Because it's very mathematical, you built a structure and then you add the dialogue and everything else. Do you find more freedom in loosening up with the structure, and specifically to this play?

Neil: You may know that better than me. And I'm not saying that. Someone who looks at it all together. I'm a bit more of a shark that way, going forward and saying I'm on to the next piece, this is what I want to do. I look at them all the time—all the time that sounds a little weird. I gotta give it to them one by one. I knew where I was going. I knew what the transformation was going to be. I knew that at some point it was going to lead to a reveal of something or if it looked like a romantic comedy or if it was turning into something of a thesis on art but I couldn't talk too much about art throughout or we might see my sleight of hand . . . it's a kind of a three card monte game you're playing with the audience and ultimately you need to turn a play in on itself to look at the audience, and the audience was here to see the play which needs to become her audience so that she can talk to them and break the fourth wall. So there's a couple things structurally that you know you have to do. You gotta set them up for yourself. and I kind of like equations like that. You know, if I'm like okay—these are gonna be three monologues but each one is gonna be this, and I like the notion of things like that. They're not so much games as they're just, I'm giving myself somewhere—you know—a playpen to work within. So I knew those things about that play. I knew I had something to say about, again, about the way we are willing to let ourselves change for someone and what people will do to other people, you know, not just women, but often a woman could look at a guy and say, "If I could just change these couple of things about that guy, that would be so great, he would be perfect," and so it had the sense of that, but ultimately, it had this artistic edge to it. Because when I first thought of the play, catalysts for it was I had done a movie called *In The Company of Men*, a few critics had asked me, what would happen if you changed the sexes, could it have been two women doing this to one man? And I thought, "Yeah." The impetus of that is kind of the pack mentality of guys, and the hunt of getting someone and how they feel about someone when they have them. So if it happened, it would be a woman who played two guys off against each other or you know, I had a different notion on it. But I was thinking, what would that woman look like? So I saw this girl. And then the artistic side of it came in London working on something and I was seeing there were a lot of artists around 2000, 2001 that were not so much using people, but often using themselves in their work, and this kind of artistic work, like Marina Abramovic. There was a guy in London who took, I don't know how many pints of his own blood and then sculpted himself, sculpted a bust of himself out of his frozen blood, and then kept it in a refrigerated podium so that you could see this thing over and over. There is an artist, Tracey Emin, who uses a lot of other people in her work. She won the Turner Prize for a sort of recreation of her bedroom, basically. You walked into a studio space and there was her carpet and there was her bed and [gestures to the floor], those were her socks, and there was a used condom. She is not a very great cleaner apparently. And the interesting artistic thing is—is that art or is that someone's bedroom? If moved into an artistic space, therefore, apparently, it's art.

But for me, I had opinions about that, but what is more interesting is how subjective the whole thing was. One part of the exhibit of hers was, she often does quilting and hand painting works in neon, but they're all provocative things or drawings that she's done. She did a pop tent—you go out camping, right, that you zip up and go inside. Inside, she had sewn these patches of the names of every person she has ever slept with. I don't know if she cleared it with them or not, you're on the tent whether you like it or not. So I went in and I took my name off, slightly outraged that it was so far down, or what that meant, starting with the top . . . whose that guy? You know what I'm talking about. So you know, that wouldn't actually happen, but the tent happened, and so that made me feel, you know those people

Neil LaBute Interview

who incorporate themselves and or other people because that's their art and the peripheral damage of that, how much do they take into account? So that was what I was interested in. Could I mold those two ideas together?

Cosmin: I was going to ask about the research you did but you just answered my question.

Neil: Perfect.

Cosmin: Let's talk about *Some Girls*.

Neil: Which ones?

Cosmin: You're probably going hear this for the first time but we're planning on doing this play at Pace.

Neil: Awesome, fantastic!

Cosmin: And we're working on getting the rights right now.

Neil: I can help.

Cosmin: And—

Neil: That would be so weird if I can't help.

Cosmin: What was the moment you said you needed to write a play about that?

Neil: I'm not talking about *Some Girls*, not writing a play about some girls, I'm talking about the subject theatrically. So the beds are—there is one bed, and then they separate, and the pictures over the bed change, and so it was a very theatrical element that you could change to go "Oh look, how clever, changing it to be a new hotel room, yet it's just one set." So I love that whole idea of it. But I love the idea of somebody who goes on a kind of confessional tour . . . you know, before they move on with their life they have to take care of their past. And a person who goes ostensibly to make reparations with people, but basically, it just reopens wounds. And that person is ultimately also a writer. So where does the writer fit into life, you know? What is ours? I had an exchange with you, you know, whoever writes to make a play about this now because we spoke about it, or if you tell me something about your grandparents—is that just open season because you told me, so now I can just go write that play? Those kind of things really interest me. Partly because I made the writer a weird hybrid. A lot of the places he mentions are places that I grew up around or places that I've been, and yet the complete opposite kind of writer that I am. Because I don't pull from life. I don't like, write about my parents from when they were young or about my brother. So, I'm always just looking to make up a story. So I like the idea that someone could just read and go, "This must be about him," but actually it had nothing to do with me, yet it was about a writer. And so, all of those two-person scenes where people—man or woman—are getting down to their relationship. So it was a good leaping off place for a number four, originally four, but I added a fifth section for these nice little duets between people. And how much can you pack into twenty minutes about two people? Ultimately a lot. You know if you get right down to the heart of the matter which is, someone's been left, and there's been a breakup and you follow the thread of someone to see the damage they've done, but they didn't mean to. I'm very interested in those people.

Cosmin: And because you're not . . . let's say, are you the type of writer . . . do you find your relationship with your character evolving over time?

Neil: I don't know what you mean by that.

Cosmin: Before you create. Let's say the play is done. You obviously live in that world. You create, you put yourself in that . . .

Neil: But it's not the world I find myself living in.

Cosmin: No, not the real world—

Neil: Right.

Cosmin: The imaginary world. And then you create some sort of relationship with or place yourself in it.

Neil: I think you always do because you don't know them very well in the beginning.

Cosmin: How about after the play's over. Do you find them?

Neil LaBute Interview

Photo by Scott Wynn

Neil: I hope that I have realized them well enough to not only be playable, that actors can put them onstage that an audience wherever, Krakow or here, can really distinguish those places—ultimately it will just end up working in those two cities, here and Krakow—but that an audience can understand, but ultimately that I have humanized them. In a way that I haven't judged them. Again not having thought of them as a bad person or good person but a person who does stuff and they react to it accordingly. So I certainly know them better by the time I get through, actors tend to know them better than I do when they're done because they have lived in it a little more, filled in all the blanks. I tend to write in the here-and-now a lot.

People will talk about what happened in the past and all that but there is a lot of getting plunged right into something, so after it kind of has to go, "OK, so this is what got me here and this is what brought these two together," and I like to leave room for that. For many possible roads that got you to the moment you walk on stage. I prefer that. I prefer not to be too prescriptive. That it is, in fact, willfully oblique, that it's like, "It could be this or it could be that; I'll let you decide."

I've worked hard to leave it in the gray-zone of—it's up to you. So I think that's good for an audience, too, sometimes, as well.

Cosmin: Do you find yourself taking sides? Once in a while?

Neil: Sure. You kind of have to but you have to jump back and forth. It's like playing chess, where you have to play both sides.

Cosmin: Have you ever been [criticized] by the other side?

Neil: You mean the feminists?

Cosmin: Yeah.

Neil: I try to see all sides of the character. You have to. Not that I feel there is a little bit of me in each of these, but I have to try and—the same way I think actors try and not to judge—they get cast in something, and they try to find a way and play that person . . . it's not up to me. The audience comes in and sits back and watches, and passes a kind of judgment on them. They fill in that other side of the equation. But for me, the job is to create an interesting and challenging connection between people and a direct conflict that makes one want to find out what happens. It's moment to moment—I have to keep making the audience want to see what happens next. And that gets them to the end of the play. They don't have to love the characters, these people aren't real, you don't have to marry them, you know, you don't have to care to see them again, but you have to want to know where they're going to go. Why they made the next choice. You have to want to make the journey with them. So that's the job. To really be able to sit down and create someone who is watchable, you know? That's not everybody. I've seen many plays where I go, "I wish I had that time back," cause I didn't care in the sense that I just didn't care to know what happened. It wasn't that they made choices that I wouldn't make or they were from a culture that I didn't understand. It was just that I didn't really care whether they lived or died or whatever they did and that's the kind of cardinal sin you can't commit.

Neil LaBute Interview 71

Cosmin: What's your best piece of advice for an artist who is 18 or 19 or 20? We have a lot of actors, directors, designers, dancers. What would your advice be for today? Not for a year ago or five years ago.

Neil: It would probably be the same as something from years ago. It would probably be, "Don't take no for an answer." That was one of the best things—I mean, it would probably be different for each of those disciplines, but for directors one of the best things for me has been to be willing to say you don't know. Don't always feel like you have to know everything and be in control. I have found many actors and crew members—people appreciate when you're honest and when you show that vulnerability. That you're willing to find out, that you don't know everything ahead of time. But just in general, I had to forge my own way most of the time because of where I came from and just from being in school and there not being enough places to do plays, you know. If someone said "Nah, I can't give you any space to work in the black box," I was like, not that I was hounding until I got into the black box, but I mean in the greater sense of that doesn't mean I can't do this play, you're just telling me I can't get a space in here. And after exhausting every faculty member, who would see me coming—"Holy fuck, I gotta get out of here"—you know, "Oh, he is gonna ask about the stupid black box again."

Cosmin: Who was it then?

Neil: This was at University of Kansas for instance, that was a big problem. There wasn't enough space. So I was like "I got a play, I'll do something" and they're all like "We got a lot of students, you know, take it easy . . . relax, captain, and you'll get your one shot in there." But that wasn't enough for me. And if I couldn't find anything in the department, I was suddenly scavenging across campus. And I was doing plays under the stairwells of the Natural History Museum and clearing out spaces in residence halls. I would go down to the storage levels and put a show on and then I would go into the library—it was kind of the first good library also where I could get my hands on texts from all over the world. And I would go find a play that would fit in that space. And I'm like, "OK, now I've got a great old stairwell and I'll put the audience on those stairs and have playing space and put one light bulb up in there and power source that off their outside lamp and they won't know and now I've got a theatre." And so I'd read *The Dumb Waiter* again or I'd find a play that could fit in that space.

So that was me not taking no for an answer. I will do a play. If I don't use that space then I'll find another place. But in the general sense it was . . . If I want to do something, I'm going to find a way to do something. And it was always constantly checking and working on levels of where I set the bar for success for myself. I wanna do this, I wanna be a writer, I wanna direct, so does that mean I'm gonna go straight to New York or Broadway . . . probably not. So I'm just gonna keep doing what I do best and put it in front of an audience and get that reaction and then calibrate accordingly. And so piece by piece by piece I just kept banging away.

Cosmin: My last question and then we will turn it over to the students. Do you consider yourself in your heart more of a writer or more of a director?

Neil: I don't have a heart. I mean, mine was heavy, I was carrying it around, it wasn't doing me any good, so I said fuck it, I'm taking it out. If you put me to the task of do I have to choose one, I would choose writer. I started out doing that, and I think it's the most natural expression of what I do. I love directing, it's a different thing, it gets me out of the house. You can really easily get stuck inside, watching TV, you know, make your own hours, I still do a lot of writing that is just for me. Not that I'm only gonna read it, you know, but I mean that I don't know where it is gonna be. I don't know if anyone's gonna put it on. I haven't been commissioned by Lincoln Center or apparently English or whatever that accent just was.

But I write because I'm a writer. I have a story and I can't get rid of it. And now I have the access to a lot of people I could show it to and maybe it would get done, but I didn't think that way when I was sitting down writing it, I wrote it. I can't help myself. It's a little bit of a red shoe, you know? It's like "Oh damn, I've got something to write, I've got to write and write and write and now I've got a script." And I like to play with it and keep working on it. So it's now the directing impulse. It's a strong one but I don't think it's the same. You know, it's really—if I had to choose, it would probably be writer.

Cosmin: Great. Our students know a lot about your work. And I'm going to turn it to you guys [gestures to audience] because I want to make sure you get enough time to ask the questions you want to ask. Please feel free to step forward. We will begin the questions now.

AM (Audience Member): My name is Miranda, I'm a senior Acting major here. I'm also an aspiring writer. And I'm wondering when you started out writing, and how did you get your work shown to people? Did you get people to read it or did you put it up yourself? Did you show it to friends?

Neil: It was never an either or . . . necessarily. It's always great when you have an advocate, whether it's an agent or friend or whoever. Some access to a place that does these things is best. But in terms of theater, it was always less expensive. You know, I never really thought about making movies until I made one. Because I didn't grow up in a house that had like a Super 8 camera, and you know we didn't want to take pictures of our family, we didn't want to remember. So I didn't have that thing to go off and make little movies, and movies were very expensive back then to make—relatively, now it's easier to go off and make movies. Everyone has a camera on their phone, it's never been a better time to wanna make movies and people who are willing to watch shit on their phone and computer and so, the theatre—it doesn't take a lot, you can do 'em in the living room. You know, it just depends what is that theater to you? I hear people say "I just went and saw the Andre Gregory film." It's not really a biography, but his wife made a film about this interesting guy who was doing theater for a long time here. And he's worked for like 12 years on plays, you know that kind of thing. And he also talks about the smaller the space, the better, getting closer to the audience.

I love doing things in anything but theaters. I wanna do it in people's living rooms, that sort of thing, I love that. The smaller the better for me as well. I worked on a show that was on Broadway . . . well moved to Broadway . . . well, I think I did one that went straight to Broadway, and the whole thing kind of worries me. There's a lot of people to get in every night, big spaces, you know I like to work in miniature. I like to have people in close, where they don't feel safe. Where they aren't sitting way back there in the back. We can't even touch these people. And I like moving that safety net the audience has. So a living room is even better. So ultimately—yeah, it is great if you can find someone you know, sometimes it is a lot about who you know and the people that you meet. Oh I met someone that works at the Public Theater—maybe I can get them to show somebody this, or when I first came to New York I wanted to write . . . I could write the shit out of sketches for *Saturday Night Live*. I would look at the end of *Saturday Night Live* and see 60 people listed and I'm like, "For what? 60 people came up with that? That handful of sketches? I could write all those myself. And be as bad as that. I could be not that funny."

And so I had a friend that was an assistant for somebody. And when I visited him, I went through this guy's rolodex. And I saw he had Roman Polanski, gotta write that one down, and Lorne Michaels was in there. So I was like maybe we should cold call Lorne Michaels, see what happens. Cause you can't even get up there at NBC, you gotta go down and get on those tours. And I'm like, I got an idea. Let's call Lorne. I called him on a Sunday afternoon. Called his house. And he answered. I'm like, "Hey, uh, Lorne Michaels . . ." and I explained who I was and what I wanna do and stuff and he's like "Don't ever call this number. Don't ever call me at home." And now I'm thinking back . . . probably not the best idea. But I thought, you know, whatever it takes to make this happen. Maybe he'll appreciate the chutzpah of doing it. And he asked me to send him some stuff and I did and never heard from him. I met him years later and we had a good laugh about it because he was like, "Yeah I remember that. I remember you calling. I was like 'Don't call me at home and how'd you get my number?'" and I was like ". . . uh . . . yeah . . . I went through someone's rolodex . . . uh . . .yeah."

To me, it's like you do what you gotta do. How much do you love it? You now have 10 pages you want to put in front of an audience. Well, you send it out, you send it out to the *Drama Sourcebook*, you send it out to all of those one-act play festivals, I got so many rejections from so many places. I put them all on a "I'll fucking get you one day" list and I've gone down that list and they now ask me for plays and I go, "Nope, you're not getting a play from me ever." So I have that list. And you try out all that stuff and it's not gonna stop me either. And ultimately—the first section—I did this play called *Bash* a few years ago that has three one-act plays. The first time I ever did one of those plays was in a living room, in London, for a group of Mormons, who in the play are Mormon characters. And there were only 15 or 20 people there, and we had actors sitting by candlelight reading this play. And afterwards they were like, very nice people—"Okay, maybe we should pray, you know, for your soul . . ." essentially was what they were saying. But that was a great experience. It was so close, and I knew it was gonna mean something particular for them. And I didn't wait for ensemble theater to do it. Because if they said no, that wasn't gonna stop me, I was gonna find a place to do it. And then somebody else hears about it and we do it in somebody else's living room or find a place and it gets into a festival. And you just keep plugging away. You just have to keep at it. You have to have thick skin, and not embrace rejection, but—they aren't rejecting you—I mean it's harder for actors—actors, I don't know how you do it. Cause you go in and they're like . . . well they're saying to you "I don't want you," you know, this is your play. This is like "I don't need whatever… you are." You know, that's hard. You are what you have to offer. And you gotta be tough to go in there.

I really admire . . . I love actors. You know, I love what they do. I don't do it. It's kind of magical how they bring these things to life and especially having made some movies, people shoot 'em in such crazy ways. It's not for the actors, it's for the money. It's like, we shoot this way, because it costs us the least amount of money to make it this way. And you hope to make the most amount of money. It's all economics. It's all based on this model. Theater is a little different. You start from the beginning, and then the end, and put the show on and ask the audience to come in. But where that audience is or where you do it, it's up to you. For a while, you still have control over that. Once you hand your play off to somebody or sell a film script, they can take that and run with it, but it's just what you're willing to do, you know, and how you're willing to go about it and consider that a theatrical experience. So don't give up is the thing, you know, it's like you will hear "No" or "That sucks." You know, don't go on Twitter.

On stage at the Schimmel Center. *Photo by Scott Wynn*

Neil LaBute Interview

Don't look. It's a minefield, you know, of heartbreak. "You suck!" Thank you John79. You know it's a freedom to just do whatever you want, but you do you have to be strong enough to go, "He probably doesn't mean sucks, I mean you know, he is probably just kidding around." You've got to be true to yourself. You know when you've done something good; you know when you've done something bad. So it's a little bit like Jiminy Cricket, really, you've got your own little compass there that tells you what you're doing that's good or bad.

AM: Thank you.

Cosmin: Next question.

AM: Hello I'm Shari.

Neil: Hi Shari.

AM: I'm an acting major, I was just wondering, were your childhood storybooks that you wrote happy? And also, when did you start really thinking about people's dark sides?

Neil: I'm sure there was some happiness in those stories and there is some happiness in the stories I still write so I can't remember, I wish I had a few of them still, I don't think my mom kept necessarily anything like that, but you know, the job of the writer is one in which you create conflict. Depending on how much, that's up to you, and depending on the writer, but without it you don't really have drama. If you have a couple together and the man is really into the woman and the woman kind of feels the same way and the sun is shining and you don't have to go to work. "Let's just hang out and just be together and we'll eat dinner." You know what? You don't have a play, you don't have anything, you have a happy couple, God bless them, and go on your way. But that's not who I'm not looking for. I'm looking for that person who has made another kind of decision, or is harboring a secret, or is you know, has just done something they are going to regret, or they are just about to fall in love, but unfortunately they are actually married to somebody else. That's what I'm looking for, you know, then you've got something you can work with that you can just begin to feel around for the cracks of where that thing is going to fall apart.

So it's not so much the dark side, it's just you have to, you have to be willing to go where those stories take you and most of the stories, whether there is comedy in them or not, someone has to want something and someone else has to want the same thing and wants to take it from them or wants something else and they have to constantly be either ramming into each other or one running from the other. That's my job—to create a shitty day for someone. Happily most of those people are fictional. But that's what I'm supposed to do. That's what you ultimately pay money to go see is not a bunch of people who are all pretty well-adjusted and pretty happy with everyone around them. It's just not, it's certainly not how I understand it works and or the kind of thing I want to write. I'm sure that exists somewhere, but it's not what I want to do.

AM: Thank you.

Cosmin: Who's next?

AM: Hello I'm Aaron, I'm a junior BFA Acting major.

Neil: Hi Aaron.

AM: My question is, in your experience as a director all over the world, which project was your favorite experience with a group of actors and what did they bring to that project that changed it for you and that made it your favorite and how did that affect the rehearsal process and how that project grew to the performance?

Neil: You know I have been lucky enough to have a few of those, actually. But I guess the best experience I had wasn't with a group of people but it was with one actor. I did this show, it was a one man show called *Wrecks* with Ed Harris and it started it started in Cork, Ireland. We had an invitation to go there and we did it there. We did it at the Public Theater here and we did it twice in Los Angeles. Once in an auditorium, maybe this size, and then once in like a hundred seat theater. So every time we did it the space kept getting smaller

Neil LaBute Interview

and it was great. By the last time we did it, he was this close to the audience, because he also breaks the fourth wall because it's a monologue and it's not, you know, it's not him talking to one person, so he can talk to the entire group. And he is just a phenomenal actor and great person and so honest and that's really what spikes his acting. You know you just always knew every day where he was, how he felt, what he was thinking, and it just seeped over into his work. And to watch him was a real pleasure, you know, it was great that it was my words in his hands, but more than that I just enjoyed watching the guy work and how he dealt with an audience. How charming he was, how sharp, how precise everything was. How he could roll with a moment if something happened, you know, fantastic.

You know, I don't know what the ingredients are that make it work. . . was it that it was one person, but it was just one of those things that the script just worked, a perfect match for him. It was over the course of like five years that we did that, too; it was just like, leaving here and going here, that was the run. We would talk and say, "Hey somebody else wants to see the show, let's do it again" and we'd remount it and do it. So we got together like four times over the course of five years to do this and I was excited to go back every time just because I knew what I was gonna be doing. But inside the room with people who want to be there, who wanna do good work, doesn't mean in the end it's going to be a great show, but everybody is there for the right reason. I've had the opposite experience. I've done a play, not very many, but I've done at least one play in this city where the show—I was happy with the product, happy with the show, but hated the experience. The director was a pain in the ass and we had an actress who was a real problem, who ultimately got replaced, and all for the wrong reasons, all for, you know, ego driven, really just kind of like, why is this happening? I never felt good about it, as good as the play turned out. I always kind of held a grudge against that experience because the process was ruined. I love going to work, every day I like going to work. I'm lucky enough to work in something that I want to do. Some days are good, some days are bad. "Oh god, I hope I get this, oh I didn't, oh the reviews were bad. Fuck, I don't care."

I love doing this and I've done a lot of other jobs. I taught, which I really liked. I've done a ton of other just work—work jobs. From working on a farm, to unloading box cars, to all kinds of shit and those were hard jobs that I was like, "Yeah, you know what I've learned from this is that I don't want to do this for the rest of my life." And so I love the process of theater and films and all that so and I hate being around people who don't like it yet profess to like to do it. That he understands when he doesn't do it, and you kind of look at what you do, like weird hours, don't like the people, they're kind of strange. I thought the movies would be cool, you guys just sit around and talk a lot. You know, all while they are eating food. But you know, I understand, if you don't understand it you don't understand it. You don't have to like it, you don't have to love it, but when you say you wanna do it, that you like doing theater and then something about it bothers you every day, it's weird, it's a weird thing to me. I think when you're lucky enough to do what you set out to want to do, you should be thankful. So you know, and most times you are just lucky to be there as well. So much of what will happen to you in your lives and certainly in your jobs will be based on luck. You know, who you meet, that you're ready when the opportunity comes — "But god, I never expected it to be today." You'll have understudied something for a year, and you're like "Ugh, I just have to go to the theater, oh someone called me and said you're going on tonight." This is it, I'm ready and people see it and go, "Who is that person?"

It happens, you know those kind of wonderful things still happen in this life, so, you can prepare yourself so much and then sometimes it's just the miracle of, you know, of living. And so that's hopefully something that everybody who does this, you know you're here for the right reason, because you love it in the end. You can't imagine really doing something else. I've always kind of lived that way. Another piece of advice I would give is to get into the mindset of

"It's a matter of when, not a matter of if." I've seen lot of people fall by the wayside, you know, I have gone to school with a lot of good students, I've taught good students who ultimately gave up. They said, "You know I gotta get a law degree. I gotta have something that I know that I'm gonna get a paycheck on, I can do this" and you know there is still some sort of performance. I'm still a liar essentially. I'm just paid for it on a regular basis. And I get it but they allowed it to exist and I always had the mindset, when it was very hard times and when you know even now that, you know, it was when it was going to happen not if it was going to happen.

AM: Thank you.

Neil: You're welcome.

Cosmin: We have time for two more questions. Thomas.

AM: My name is Thomas, I'm a BA Acting Major but I wanted to ask you something about *Fat Pig*.

Neil: Yes.

AM: I wanted to ask you about what do you want, you know for an actor, what would you like for them to bring to the sort of predatory dynamic of Tom and Carter?

Neil: Well, it's a particular world to work in business, you know, I didn't do a lot of work in business, but I've been around a lot businesses. I worked for a software company for a while and I would go to different businesses, so I could see a lot of kinds of business. The dynamic is a very interesting one, so I've written about business a few times in a very general way. I always like businesses where you have no idea what the fuck is going on. They're always just talking about stuff. Guys are kind of hanging out in their office. You know the business seems to be going on elsewhere. As in life sometimes, I often make the male character sitting around doing nothing and getting more—better paid than the women who are actually working, because these things actually happen in life sometimes, you know.

So Carter is an animal, he works the room beautifully, you know. I've seen him played as a, you know, the kid brother. I've seen him played as the older brother. The very slick friend. The kind of aggressive, you know, fraternity brother. I've seen it, there is always that kind of element, when you know it can go in a number of ways. But I think he's a guy you make friends with in the office because it would be worse to not be his friend. But not someone that you really ultimately care about in life. That guy, that's not the guy I'm gonna call in an emergency. Hey, he would be great in an emergency, but it's just you're friends by convenience, but we happen to work here and he keeps coming into my fucking office. You know, I never go to his office; he just comes to my office. And so we hang out and talk and sometimes we play basketball and you know, but that's the kind of relationship that they have. You know, the play was kind of one thing and then ultimately I found that it was studying weakness, it was a study of cowards. You know, when it works well and I've seen one actor who did it,

I've see a couple of actors do it really well. I've see an actor who didn't get it, who didn't get the essential, because he didn't fall in love with Helen. There is only really one scene in the play where you have to see that he loves Helen. When they are alone together and that, "You know that I love this girl. You know, I've been out with other girls. The girl in the office that I used to date is conventionally pretty and she's got a good figure. That's not who I'm supposed to be with. You know. I haven't quite like, apparently broken up with her, so I, you know, didn't do the right thing. Therefore shit is happening to me at this moment, but I meet this other girl and I love her and yet I'm so concerned about what everybody else thinks that I can't stand up for what I believe in." Ultimately, when the play happened, the first production of it, I realized what was working with audiences. It wasn't, you know, that they enjoyed Helen and they liked this guy, seen some cast members, you know, in projects before, but wasn't just the story of Helen and Tom, but they could see often themselves, because everybody had, most people as adults have had some variety of relationships. They could say I know what they are going through. I had a friend or I've done this. When somebody has been with someone else that they weren't comfortable letting the world know about it so they try to keep the two worlds essentially operational. My private life and my public life and when those collide, you have your conflict. And so this was a guy who had to, in his heart, know this is the girl for me.

You know, I'm not going to go as far as saying they would be together forever, that's not my concern. My concern is, I love her, in the moment I have fallen in love with her, but is it love if you can't stand up for your conviction? Can you stand up for your love? If you go, "I don't want to introduce you to people because they'll think you're, ugg." So that guy is weak. I don't hate him, he doesn't really piss me off. I'm more sorry for him than anything. I just look at him and go "You're weak" and it probably triggers what is weak inside me. You know it makes me want to be better than that. And I'm necessarily not better than that, but those are interesting people who actually can stand up for their convictions. Who, in war, or in court, or in Congress or wherever have been able to stand up and say this is what I believe. You know particularly, when you get into life-or-death situations then you're talking about real heroism. But even here is a guy who, you know, ultimately, why does he fucking care if Jamie or Carter or the whole company doesn't like who he goes out with? But he admits I don't, I don't even know why, but I do and I can't deal with it and so I'm gonna have to let you go. And I found that really kind of sad, interesting, realistic situation and so I think that a person has to bring that to the table. They bring a lot of charm, a lot of it, but they have to be all in love with that girl and then in the end they don't have the spirit to stand by it.

AM: I'm a huge fan, thank you very much.

Neil: Thank you.

Cosmin: Our last question.

AM: Hi my name is Gabe.

Neil: Hey Gabe.

AM: Did you ever have an idea that you didn't feel like you could do it justice, and then run into a play, or perhaps an idea, that you're thinking but you feel you actually aren't ready for?

Neil: Good question. I think anything can be written about. That's a slightly more general side of what you're asking but I think any subject is open season. I don't think anything is taboo. This is the place to do it. On stage, in fiction. It's a good safe place to work out these things and to talk about everything. Desires and, and fears, hopes and dreams, and all that stuff. All that shit, like hopes and dreams. Sometimes yeah, I'm not the right person for the job. I don't always know that until I get to the end. Sometimes not even until the play has been produced, you know, or a movie has been made. I can think of one example at least.

Photo by Scott Wynn

One of the plays that I worked the hardest on, wrote the largest number of drafts, you know, really kept at it scene after scene after scene—I felt I never got quite right. Kind of got away from me. Great idea, happy that I did it, but I don't think I ever got it exactly right. Maybe somebody else would. I don't know. But it was my idea, you know, and I didn't know ultimately until I saw it produced, a couple of times, that I went, "I don't know if I got that right. Don't know if it was the structure or if it was the idea, or what it was." I tried blaming it on other people naturally, but in the end I kind of go, "Yeah, don't think I ever got it." But I didn't feel like I wasn't the right person for it. I just ultimately didn't get it right. I don't know, five years from now, that I would get it any more right, you know. But I was too close to it or I just didn't get that one, you know. I was talking about, like the 9/11 piece, I had a couple of people, more than a couple, say, more than a couple, say "Too soon. We shouldn't write anything about 9/11, we shouldn't write that kind of play." People don't wanna remember it in that way. But, I didn't even think twice about that at the time. I was like, "I have the idea; I am going to write this. I'm not writing any specific person, any one's actual situation. I'm just using it as a backdrop for something." So I never felt like, "Oh, I can write about that, people will be irritated that I did that or that I'm making money off of a national tragedy." Never enters my mind. But I don't think that it filters through me. Maybe I'll need to be that much more mature to be able to handle it or just will have lived that much more. I don't think that's the case for me.

AM: You'd say it's ok to say no to some things then?

Neil: Oh god yeah. I mean, yeah, I say no all the time and people say no to me, and that's OK. I mean, I don't think as an actor you have to go out there and take everything that comes your way. It's great to get experience, but is it great to be in something bad? Sometimes, sometimes it is because you learn a lot from it. You know, I've learned a lot from the things that have not gone as well as the things that have gone well. If I could write, you know, a musical, I still probably wouldn't. But the dramatic theater, you know—everything's not in the same ball park. I do theater because I love it and occasionally I get paid and sometimes I get paid well, but it really is almost nothing to do with that. So yeah, I think it's great, you know, it's work, I think of this as my job. Roll up your sleeves. You're not going to get a script unless you sit your fat ass down and write a script. You can talk about it, you can sit in Starbucks and let people think you're a writer or you can sit down and write the fucking thing—write it! And that's ultimately what I learned you had to do.

You know, it didn't matter where you were sitting or what time of day, you know. You could be in prison, or you can be on the campaign trail, or you can be a housewife or whatever. Those are really the only three jobs. So take your pick. You can write if you want to write. You can find the time. If you have to wait until midnight when your child goes to sleep or when you get off your job or when you use your break time when you're supposed to be eating lunch. You've got one hand with a sandwich and the other hand is writing. You can find time to write and the pages will pile up. I met a lot of people who said they're writers and fewer who actually show me scripts and even fewer still from that group who actually want me to tell them the truth about their script. Most of them want you to say it's good. So now I just ask, "If you want me to just say it's good I will. I don't even have to read it, I'll just say it to make you feel better. But if you want to know the truth, then I want you to tell me the truth, then let's get into a different conversation." Sometimes you have to do other things, people have to eat, people have to work, and I get that, but the more often you can do that thing you have something to say about, I think all will be better off, the whole process will grow from that.

AM: Thank you

Cosmin: I know you guys have more questions and you'll get a chance to ask more questions in about twenty minutes when we have the book signing in the lobby. But before that I wanted to say that Neil brought a little surprise for us, two short films that he wrote and one of them he directed.

Neil: I directed the first one.

Cosmin: Would you mind introducing the first one?

Neil LaBute Interview

Neil: The first one is called *Sexting*. it's with Julia Stiles and it's something we shot in a couple of hours in Los Angeles, probably two years ago now, and it was a monologue that I had written and she was gonna perform and make a film out of it. So we built a framework for it and that's what you'll see here.

Cosmin: It'll take a second to upload. There we go.

[Video plays.]

[Audience applauds.]

Cosmin: How many takes for the first scene?

Neil: The monologues, that's what we wanted to do, Julia and I had worked on a benefit for MCC, just before that and we talked about doing something together, film wise, and you know someone who does a lot of film I think they often lose that sense of, just having that freedom to perform. You know you do so many takes you have to worry about the continuity of the cigarette and all of that shit. So it's always nice to just be given the freedom to work. So I said, "I promise you, the meat of that, that monologue, I'll shoot that in one take. It'll just be a long take and I wanna use that so we got to get the whole thing right and I'll build the framework around it." You know, coming in, the mistaken identity and then the end. So that six-minute chunk or so that she does, we ended up probably shooting about three or four, three or four. One was recorded, we had a sound issue, and so we probably had three that were clean. This one was the most obvious to me. There was a good one that had a sound issue in it, we probably could have gotten around that, but I couldn't cut, I didn't want to cut anything out. So there was that to deal with and that was probably the second take, the first take was just probably not as strong, but we had very little time to shoot the whole thing and you always sort of start wide and move in. So we ultimately didn't end up having much time for her to shoot. She had extended her stay in L.A. to do it and she learned the thing and made it in a few hours, so we didn't have the luxury of twenty takes, it was just a few takes but I knew we had it when we walked away.

Cosmin: What's the second one?

Neil: The second one is called *Afterschool Special* and it's something that I wrote for some people to make a film out of so I wrote a script but I wasn't there when they shot the film. I've done that for a couple of different people, but it's nice to be able to write something for someone as opposed to always knowing the direction, just to see what they will do with it. But I work with them, the producer had worked in theater and he was gonna work on a short film, and so he asked me to provide some material. So this is the film that I gave him. He went off and made a film in Los Angeles.

[Video plays.]

Cosmin: That was great. Thank you.

[Audience applauds.]

How and Why to Teach Acting for Film, Television, Voice Overs, and Commercials

By Brian Hastert

In May 2017, Pace University conferred the Bachelor of Fine Arts degree on its first class of majors in Acting for Film, Television, Voice Overs, and Commercials (FTVC). It is the first major to focus entirely on the craft of acting as conveyed through the camera or microphone.

There has been a resilient bias in the world of acting and actor training which is that true artistry is earned on stage. The acknowledged path is to hone the craft on the boards and then transition those skills to the screen. The reverse path, starting with film or TV work and transitioning to the stage, is not recognized as producing successful results.

There is some history to buttress this trope. We can all name members of the long, illustrious list of actors who were trained for the theater before beginning brilliant film careers, but the list of film actors who went on to become beacons of the stage seems harder to call to mind.

Much has changed in the entertainment industry, in technology, in audience tastes, and in training methodology in this country over the last 70 years since alumni of the Group Theatre began to revolutionize the way actors learn to act. It's time to reexamine that old, resilient bias. This article is an unpacking of the choices that must be made to train actors in the digital age (no matter what kind of program you are running) and of the way we framed our choices for the Acting for Film, Television, Voice Overs, and Commercials Program at Pace School of Performing Arts.

Recruiting

Among the most bedrock questions to be addressed in creating a new actor training program of any variety is "What qualities does one look for in incoming students?" Aside from the ubiquitous-to-the-point-of-meaningless metric of talent, which means 101 different things to 101 different auditors, the FTVC program was in a position to radically investigate admittance criteria. After all, the notion of who has the potential makings of a great actor shifts in accordance with what you perceive the job requirements of actors to be. And the job of actors on screen differs in subtle but important ways from the job of actors on stage.

The audition process has been a learning curve for me in terms of what I think I'm looking for and then what winds up being useful qualities for success within the program. As one of my current students reflected while speaking to prospective students, "We're not auditioning people who are great actors. We're auditioning people who can be great students."

Because it's acting for film and TV, we don't have to look for people who have what I would call "theatrical instincts" or a theatrical level of expression. If a prospective student can express much more locally or conversationally using somebody else's words in a way that feels truthful and honest—even if it's just from across the table—then that's a starting point. We can enhance their scale of expression over the course of our time together, but honesty of expression, more than scale, is a crucial beginning.

Additionally, we don't have to find people who look like they should be actors. We're finding people who look like they are people and if we can teach them to express fully from wherever they are, then we expand our ability to represent a wider swath of humanity in our stories. So we're not trying to fill spots or archetypes. In a way we're doing our very best to bend archetype in terms of the people who come in and the range of stories it allows us to tell when we do.

A Note About "Attractiveness"

This comes up surprisingly often in conversations about acting programs and acting students, and the FTVC program is no exception. So I'd like to address it in the context of recruiting.

How and Why to Teach Acting For Film

The common observation is that actors as a group tend to be a bit more "attractive" on the whole than the population at large. I have been asked many times by men and women how much "attractiveness" is a part of admission consideration. It does, after all, seem to be a part of the job description for it affects employment prospects after graduation. The often unspoken, but understood assumption is that it affects employment prospects in unfair, biased, subjective, and sexist ways. So should it factor into admissions? Particularly for on-camera actors?

First of all, discussing this at all feels very much like engaging in the very objectification of young women and men that we denounce when applied to ourselves and, as such, it makes me personally very uncomfortable. It is simultaneously a fact of the industry that looks and appearance are part of what you are marketing as an actor and it is impossible and foolish to try to shield the students from that forever, *and also* that we as educators must work very hard to acknowledge this phenomenon without ever appearing to endorse this system or play within its rules.

Second of all, I have a theory of relative attractiveness to offer up and it goes like this: Being observed is a stressful act for a lot of people (more on this later). It tenses up the subject of observation, and that tension gets re-manifested in the bodies of the observers in the silent mirroring in which audiences constantly participate. You can't rest your eyes on them because it affects them, which in turn affects you. It creates a discomfort feedback loop that is only broken once the observer departs.

Actors are people who are trained to resist that tensing up, resist that denial of access, and embrace being witnessed. This puts the viewer at a kind of ease, and I think that's what we believe is attractive about them. Over the course of the time here, one of the grounding elements of the physical portion of the training is considerable work with the Alexander Technique and Klein Technique which are all about finding those habitual tensions and residual resistances in your body, locating and becoming aware of them, and then learning how to make new choices when you spot them. So it's not about hating that aspect of yourself but understanding that it's there and learning how to make a choice and let that go and to be more fully present. A big part of that element gets introduced in the sophomore year of the FTVC program. I would say between the beginning and the end of sophomore year the students become more visible within their own skin. This, to me, is a major function of what we call the "attractiveness" of actors.

Training Foundation

The Hawthorne Effect and Truth on Camera

The camera does not suffer artifice or "performance." Narrative storytelling on camera, for film or television or even commercials, does not seek to ask audience members to suspend their disbelief in the same way that theater does. The circumstances may be fantastic, the effects may be other-worldly, but the humanity must appear authentic, alive, and real no matter how extraordinary the moment.

How does the audience perceive realness? There is the dialogue, of course, as there is in theater, and that must give the illusion of spontaneity. But in film there is also a lot of storytelling driven by images, silent interaction with other characters and environments. What is an actor doing in those moments if not speaking dialogue? Listening. Thinking. Pursuing his or her desires in the way people have since time immemorial—without language.

It is tempting to think, therefore, that the first step in training actors for the camera is to teach them how to talk and listen in believably spontaneous ways. But from the first day of class they show up and talk and listen and respond to my questions and to each other in completely believable and spontaneous ways. I am utterly fooled into thinking that they have not rehearsed the way they say hello as they enter the classroom or the ums and stutters as they offer feedback to their peers. They are already so authentic and alive. What is left to teach?

It turns out that the results are not so universally believable when we ask them to speak specific text given to them instead of whatever they'd like to say. The results get even less believable when we ask them to speak specific text in response to something specific. But why is that? What is functionally so different about the act of listening and responding in class (or at work or on the subway) and listening and responding when the text of your answer is given to you?

We know from our high school physics classes that, at least in terms of subatomic particles, the act of observation physically alters the thing being observed. In order to observe, to watch, to record, we must apply an energy of our own. There is no such thing as passive observation, at least in the world of physics. But if that feels too true not to be a metaphor for human behavior, you're onto something. Researchers looking for ways to increase worker productivity at the Hawthorne Works factory in Illinois discovered that by turning up the lights in the factory, productivity increased. Productivity also increased when they later dimmed the lights. Productivity increased with every adjustment they made. The result was baffling until the researchers' own light bulbs blinked on and they realized that each adjustment they made signaled to the workers that they were being watched. The workers were subconsciously adjusting their behavior under scrutiny. Observation affects performance (Zaleznik).

The Hawthorne Effect is an invaluable starting place for actor training. Every student, regardless of level of experience or prior training, is going to come in with certain performance ticks. In this context, I'm using "performance ticks" to mean the habituated physiological responses that arise in actors under the scrutiny of observation. The pressure of being actively observed is the key catalyzing agent that will reveal these habits. Many students will complain that their private rehearsals were great! Much better, freer, more spontaneous, etc., than their work in class. What actor among us hasn't experienced this? Isn't every burgeoning singer's singing better in the shower than in front of judgmental crowds?

The types of ticks that surface will vary widely from person to person, but there seem to be some consistent motifs. We might offer some recurring discoveries and typical technical adjustments listed below. But before we get into what notes we give, first we must talk about the philosophy behind the giving of notes for the greatest possible chance of enhancing a student's ability to perform with believable spontaneity when the impediments to such freedom are often rooted deep in subconscious habit. Psychologist Patricia Devine at the University of Wisconsin-Madison (UW) has been studying racial prejudice and stereotypes for decades. She discovered that people would often answer test questions in such a way as to display a lack of prejudice, but would then reveal more prejudicial attitudes in their behavior. This seemed to be because the test questions were accessing people's conscious minds, and knowing that they were under observation and wanting to appear racially enlightened to the observers, subjects would adjust their answers to be perceived accordingly. Meanwhile the same subjects were put in situations designed to reveal attitudes through subconscious behavior like body language, and researchers detected far more prejudice than subjects were aware of or would admit to. They were documenting implicit bias.

Ms. Devine and a team of researchers have developed a system for unlearning and reducing implicit racial bias (Devine). This is relevant to our work training young actors because they are essentially defining racial bias as a series of habits, cognitive associations, and learned behaviors that have been culturally reinforced.

One of the methods Devine's team has come up with to unlearn these biases is described succinctly as "Detect, Reflect, Reject." This method can help acting students detect performance ticks, reflect on where that habit comes from and whether they believe it is serving their pursuit of spontaneous truth, and finally, reject the subconscious tick in order to substitute a more integral choice.

In an interview with Alix Spiegel of NPR (Spiegel), psychologist Will Cox, another member of the UW team, described the nature of the challenge, "Human brains are very good at learning things and not so good at unlearning things" (Cox). This is exactly why for actors, formal training (over the course of several years) is the perfect venue for this difficult, necessary work. Habits are self-reinforcing. Every time a performance tick manifests, it reaffirms the connection between the stimulus of being observed and the action of whatever the habit happens to be. Only with sustained, extremely consistent and immediate feedback can actors begin to detect when those habits kick in. Awareness is utterly crucial, and it takes time to build. Importantly, feedback must be given in a non-judgmental way. It is tempting enough to judge ourselves harshly every time we succumb to habit, but that judgment cripples our ability to detect. As an instructor, it is imperative to teach the building of awareness of habit in a judgment-free way.

Here are some common performance ticks that we've detected:
- An actor stops breathing at the end of a line of dialogue only to perform a quick "catch breath" before speaking again.
- An actor speaks in an "actor-y voice" that does not resemble his or her normal speaking voice.
- An actor's gaze may travel down or all around the room in a way that doesn't resemble their gaze in real conversation.
- An actor may unnecessarily tense parts of her or his body (ribs, legs, toes, throat, eyebrows, etc.) that remain otherwise released when the actor talks and listens in non-performative contexts.
- An actor develops a particular speech rhythm or pattern that intrudes into most dialogue, whereas their non-performance speech patterns are much freer and more diverse.
- An actor repeats dialogue in a way that sounds more or less identical from rehearsal to rehearsal, despite changes in circumstance or stimuli.

These are all habits that operate on a subliminal level and disrupt the audience's perception that they are watching a spontaneous, believable interaction. The camera is not a forgiving instrument. When it captures an actor on autopilot, behaving in accordance with performance ticks and not in accordance with the given circumstances of the story at hand, it can only pass it on to the audience as is. The inches of air between the lens and the actor's eyes do not obscure, they reveal.

Enabling the Individual Weirdness

So the first major step in on-camera actor training is teaching actors to develop awareness of performer habits in order to inhibit or reject them. When actors display a series of unconscious performer ticks, they are missing an opportunity to reveal anything special or unique about humanity through their interpretation of their character's plight. What they reveal, instead, are their learned biases about performance, and often their biases about what certain emotions look or sound like.

By steadily reducing the power of those habits, an actor is making room for his or her own individuality by way of vulnerability. The fundamental technique of the FTVC program relies on this equation: habits are a form of certainty, of security. They are the body's ready answer to particular stimuli. When an actor rejects those habits, she or he creates room for uncertainty in the body. Uncertainty embraced is the essence of vulnerability. When we create space for vulnerability in this manner, where the body and therefore the actor do not quite know what the response is but feel a need to respond nonetheless, that is where we may start to see an individual's weirdness reveal itself. A sound, a gesture, a look, an inflection, something erupts out or seethes out or burps out to address the circumstances that surround that actor that ultimately puts the audience/class more in touch with the actor/student, brings us more insight into her or his unique beating heart rather than their prowess in engaging the tropes of performance. Those strange eruptions and burps of humanity are the tiny building blocks that come together to reveal what is important to a character, through the cultivated space, for surprise, rather than the actor declaiming what is important to a character through the subconscious certainties of performance

Acting Technique for the Contemporary Actor

In the training I received both as a graduate and undergraduate, the most effective lessons were not presented to me as ascribed to the deceased person who developed those exercises. I may have been working on Stella Adler's exercises but they weren't necessarily introduced to me that way and they certainly weren't taught by her. Sanford Meisner, brilliant though he was, has been dead for a long time. Lee Strasburg has been dead for a long time, too. Stanislavski has been dead for a very long time. Did they change things? Absolutely they did, for the better mostly, although arguably not always. The best training I had was from people who took whatever they learned and combined it with whatever made sense to them on their own and then gave me that. When I learned to play actions it came from director Evan Yionoulis. She taught them to me in her vocabulary, not one that I had ever heard before, and it was the first time that playing actions had ever made sense to me. When I teach, and what I encourage in other professors, is if there's stuff in Meisner that works for them then articulate what works about it and why it's useful. If they want to use those exercises, then they should. If they can find other ways to teach the same concepts, I'm open to that. We don't owe fealty to anybody; whatever is going to help the professors reach the students and unlock something, that's the lesson of the day. I teach things that Ron Van Lieu taught me, that Evan taught me, that Louis Scheeder taught me along the way and amalgamate those things that obviously carry Stanislavski's tradition because everything about modern acting carries his tradition. But is it important that we give him a shout out when we do it? The history is valuable, but I'm not sure it's absolutely necessary for practical application and pragmatic artistic growth that we trace the lineage of an exercise or the individual components of the philosophy in the moment. We have advanced from there.

These were women and men who found aesthetic values in what they were taught, filtered what they learned through their own experience, and then tried to help other people gain access to the same aesthetic and performance values. We are doing the same thing. The aesthetic and performance values that we embrace have changed. If we were to see Odets' plays the way Harold Clurman directed them and Stella Adler and Sanford Meisner performed them, the performances may well feel a bit old-fashioned. The Group Theatre, from which most modern acting technique in America comes, is tremendously important history, but the art of acting has progressed in the last 75 years.

Here are some simple, practical ways teaching acting for the camera differs from teaching acting for the stage. In theater you want to be finding your moments, finding your life over the course of several weeks of rehearsal with a skilled director helping guide you. On film and in television that is not the case. You show up, you've already done all the work that you're going to accomplish in rehearsal. You already understand who this character is, what his or her aches are, what he or she yearns for, and then you walk in, you see the set for perhaps the first time. You have only a moment to get acclimated to it and determine how your blocking is going work on this particular set. And then you start shooting it and you have to be ready to roll immediately with everything else so firmly ensconced in you that you can be alive and reactive and let the other stuff go. So what we're teaching in class is how to do the homework, gobs and gobs of homework, so the actor is prepared for that, for how to be spontaneous, and for how to let that go very quickly.

Another major difference is the kinds of text you'll be encountering. A lot of stage-based training is about encountering the different texts of the canon. You've got Mamet, Shakespeare. Lynn Nottage--which all have their own kind of poetry. In film and television you've got to get used to the notion that the words that you use to communicate the life you've built are sparer. You're going to have fewer words to communicate at least as full a life as you would live on stage. So what do you do with all that work if it's not going to be articulated in words? Well, it turns out you have to look at life for that. People communicate with extraordinary nuance and very few words in life. While there are writers like Aaron Sorkin who will challenge actors to think and communicate in long thoughts, TV and film dialogue often emulates the verbal efficiency people find in high stakes situations. So you have to get used to living within a visual story told through twenty-four still images per second. The cinematographer and the director and the gaffer are all making choices to position you in the picture in a way in which your words expand the visual story as opposed to being the primary vehicle of the story. This changes the obligations of the actor to live within those choices as opposed to within the stage director and lighting designer's choices, where the actor's job is to tell a story with her or his words and help guide the audience's attention around the stage.

Preparing for the Market as Part of an Actor's Work, not Apart From It

Everyone understands how difficult it is to get jobs as an actor. The trope of work scarcity among actors goes back at least as far as the birth of modern realist acting, as Anton Chekhov ably displays for us in the character of Arkadina in *The Seagull*. If we as purveyors of actor training don't (a) acknowledge that for most actors, one is likely to spend much more time and energy pursuing acting work than working gainfully, and (b) go on to use the occasion of acknowledging this time-honored ratio to therefore teach the skills of getting work as part of an actor's work, then we are missing opportunities to impart invaluable and supplementary skills such as entrepreneurship and marketing, and to dig further into soft skills such as personal assertiveness and resilience.

The FTVC program at Pace School of Performing Arts addresses these issues from several angles. First, the training is designed to provide students with the opportunity to perform in front of and interact with cameras several times weekly beginning in the sophomore year. Students practice the foundational technique while learning what reads on screen and what doesn't. Students have time to become comfortable watching themselves and learning to utilize that playback to help further reduce habits and tensions while expanding their expressive repertoires.

Second, there is a steady practice of auditioning throughout the second, third, and fourth years. Auditioning must be taught to be the essence of the actors' work, not a troublesome hurdle an actor must jump in order to finally be invited to work. Like any exhibition of an actor's work, there are surrounding circumstances. Instead of a theater with hundreds of seats or a set with dozens of crew workers, it is an intimate room with a small number of people. Often a camera. And because it is a small room with a camera and people you may not know very well, the Hawthorne effect may be heightened causing defense habits and tensions to arise, baffling your best rehearsed intentions. Let us acknowledge the severity of the bias most actors carry into auditions and then devote the necessary time and care to teach them how to unlearn those biases and learn new modes of behavior so that young actors can take command of an audition room with as much confidence as a rehearsal room or closing night's show.

Third, we devote an entire semester's class to a thorough exploration of "type." This felt like the biggest gamble of all in the creation of this new program. Type can feel like such a gross concept. No one wants to be pigeon-holed or reduced. I can feel my quills go up thinking about it even now, each one stenciled with "but I'm versatile!"

Here's why it is essential to work on type. It helps to bridge the gap between the first two years of training (in which actors explore and express their individual weirdnesses, throwing off the shackles of tropes, habits, and subconscious biases in favor of honesty and surprise) and the third and fourth years (in which actors are routinely subjected to the scrutiny of industry professionals who are evaluating them to see where any individual actor may fit into a particular project or client roster). The types class is about recognizing the fact that the actor may feel one way about him- or herself but may be perceived another way. Actors in the class are taught that is an extremely common phenomenon. It is about recognizing the deep part of our human nature that begins assessing people immediately upon meeting them. When I walk into the room, you're going to have thoughts about me. You're going to look at me and assume something, or think something, or conceive of me in some way. If I can understand that this function occurs and how it occurs for me in particular then I can contribute to that. I can take some of that ownership back.

This provides a space that encourages students to explore notions of identity from several perspectives and, ultimately, take ownership. An actor must ask, "Who do I feel that I am?" and then "Who do you perceive me as?" There may be many different answers, but over time a general theme will emerge as an answer to each question. The new questions become "Can I present myself in such a way that you will see me as I see myself?" and "Can I enjoy embodying the person, the energetic archetype that I am perceived as even if I do not often identify that way? Is it in there somewhere?" By bringing different scenes into class and getting consistent feedback from classmates and the instructor, students begin to take ownership of the way they present themselves in audition and performance settings.

Conclusion

We are currently in the midst of an important shift in American storytelling. The shift is about Representation. Who gets their stories told, and who gets to tell them? Who writes them, who directs them, who produces them, and, crucially, who embodies them? Gone, blessedly, are the days when Mickey Rooney dressed in excruciatingly offensive yellow face for a major motion picture. Not gone are the days when an Asian character is played by Scarlett Johansson (*Ghost in the Shell*, 2017) and a Native American character by Johnny Depp (*The Lone Ranger*, 2013). But, importantly, those choices now come in the context of our larger national conversation about Representation and productions are forced to defend choices that diminish a more honest representation and whitewash their worlds.

More and more stories are being told that are outside the predominantly white, predominantly male, predominantly heteronormative, predominantly cisgendered, and predominantly well-to-do worlds that overrun centuries of western dramatic literature. This is an incredibly positive trend, but there is a long way to go. It creates a bigger, more complex world and allows us to find empathy for people who we may at first not recognize as worthy of it because that's what these superficial differences are capable of doing - obscuring our beating hearts from one another.

Many of these stories are being told on screens large and small. Our job, as trainers of young actors, is to prepare them to step into a story with integrity and expand our world. To enable them to own their own weirdness (for if they don't, then truly, who will?), bring it into the fictional circumstances, and do what must be done. Stories have evolved over millennia from the tales of kings and queens, to the tribulations of the privileged but problematic, to the life and times of our friends and neighbors, all the way to the illumination of the overlooked. The most we can hope is that this actor training program is a small piece of that continuing evolution. We seek to contribute to the continuum of bringing the beating hearts of real people into the great works, written and unwritten.

Works Cited

Cox, Will. Interview with Alix Spiegel. "The Culture Inside." Invisibilia, from NPR, 15 June, 2017. Web. <http://www.npr.org/templates/transcript/transcript.php?storyId=532955665>.

Devine, Patricia; et al. "Long-Term Reduction in Implicit Race Bias: A Prejudice Habit-Breaking Intervention." *Journal of Experimental Psychology*, vol. 48, no. 6, 2012, pp. 1267-1278. Print.

Spiegel, Alix. "The Culture Inside." Invisibilia, from NPR, 9 June, 2017. Web. <http://www.npr.org/programs/invisibilia/532950995/the-culture-inside>.

Zaleznik, Abraham. "The Hawthorne Effect." Harvard Business School, Baker Library, Historical Collections. Web. https://www.library.hbs.edu/hc/hawthorne/09.html.

The Triangle Game: A Practical Exercise to Introduce and Build Skills in Commitment and Ensemble

By Jessie Mills

Teaching an emerging actor to "commit," or remain present, focused, and energized, is a core tenet in performance pedagogy. Similarly, cultivating an actor's commitment to her fellow performers is critical conditioning. Regardless of an actor's skill level, talent, training ground, or method, these are essential skills to develop.

Toward that end, I detail in this article one movement-based exercise: the Triangle Game. This activity, an introductory exercise, instills commitment by training a performer's sense of urgency and impulse within ensemble work. I typically teach this game on the first day of class, both to set classroom expectations and to introduce students to the physical demands of the course.

Roots and Alterations

I first encountered the Triangle Game at The Piven Theatre Workshop in Evanston, Illinois. Created by Byrne and Joyce Piven, the Workshop's innovative and dynamic system of theatrical training is "greatly indebted to Viola Spolin and Paul Sills . . . Uta Hagen, [and] Etienne Decroux," in an "approach [that] brings together all these various strains—F theatre games, story theatre, mime and the Stanislavski Method" (Applebaum 16).

According to Joyce Piven, the Triangle Game descended from Etienne Decroux (Piven). While Decroux likely expanded this game, I believe that it was originally constructed by his teacher, Jacques Copeau, a theater practitioner whose "legacy has become so pervasive that it is in danger of becoming invisible" (Evans 137). According to Mark Evans:

> Copeau was truly innovatory in his use of games within actor training—his work . . . is perhaps the first modern example of games being employed in a professional actor training

regime. His work pre-dates that of later teachers . . . by several decades (63-64).

Copeau's games prioritize ensemble work, movement, and play. The Triangle Game promotes identical aims. My slight variation on this game retains these principles while simultaneously emphasizing commitment.

The Triangle Game

This game is a silent, movement-based exercise that contains four distinct steps: the Space Walk, the Relationships, the Dynamics, and the Triangle. Each step seamlessly bleeds into the next. My variation on the game, an urgency scale, is embedded between parts two and three.

Space Walk

Ensemble members begin by walking through the space. While this game is a non-verbal exercise, laughter and breath are encouraged. At the start of the game, I explain that students should work over the sound of my voice throughout the exercise. I instruct students to engage the space with a soft focus at first; they should try to take in the full room rather than settle their eyes on any one point. Next, I direct the ensemble to walk in "neutral." In this game, neutral means limbs unencumbered by pockets or other limitations, and at a pace that is typical and comfortable for each individual student. There is no need to match the pace or the energy of the room—not just yet. I also charge students to avoid walking in a circle, rather to bisect the full space as much as possible. I remind the company of this as often as necessary.

With the basics of the space walk in place, the instructor is welcome to add any additional calls or instructions she deems useful for the ensemble. With "neutral" established, I often use the space walk as a way to incorporate other vocabulary such as "freeze," which, in this game, is an active state of suspension. When freeze is called, students are to stop mid-stride, muscles engaged, ready to pick up at a moment's notice. A "neutral freeze" is a *passive* state of suspension, where students stop in a comfortable position, facing the instructor. Back in neutral walk, I ask students to study their ensemble during this introductory portion. Maintaining a soft focus, I prompt students to notice the main vs. "popping" colors within the space. I request that students note the general pace of the ensemble: the heaviness or lightness of the footsteps around them. I guide company members to notice breath in the space: the deepness and airiness of breathing. I urge students to discover how their ensemble moves: the swinging of limbs, the bounciness of steps, and the variety of postures.

Finally, to get the company acclimated to impulse and ensemble work, I ask the group to find the common pace of the room. I ask the ensemble to find the common footstep, the common breath, and the common energy. Once students reach a new equilibrium, I challenge the company to find a new speed, with no single person leading the change. I toss this challenge out several times, allowing the company to play with a variety of speeds, steps, and energies. Ensembles, even full of first-time performers, have a natural aptitude for this portion of the game. This first leg of the exercise is a swift introduction to active listening and ensemble work, as each individual has to adjust his or her own impulses to the needs of the company.

Relationships

As we shift focus, I call the ensemble back to a neutral walk. I ask that each person choose another member of his or her company in secret. It cannot be the instructor and it cannot be themselves. I caution that this choice should not be made apparent in any way. We deem this "Person A" for the remainder of the exercise. I task the ensemble to study their Person A while keeping the full ensemble in consideration. Without being noticed, I invite students to mimic A's walk exactly; to follow A; to stay at least twenty feet away from A; to stay within ten feet of A; five feet of A; two feet of A.

I call the ensemble back to neutral walk. I ask that each person choose a different member of his or her company, once more in secret. This time, it cannot be the instructor, themselves, or their Person A. I again caution that this choice should be invisible. Just as they did with their Person A, I challenge the ensemble to study and mimic B; to follow B; to play with proximity to B. This piece of the exercise establishes a set of relationships: ambiguous and arbitrary ones, to be sure, but relationships nonetheless. For beginning performers, this portion of the exercise may also be the first introduction to pursuing an objective. I often cite this leg of the activity when discussing the Stanislavski method later in the semester.

To transition this step to *Dynamics*, I freeze the company to set up the next, critical call: "You need to get *close* to Person A and *away* from Person B. Go!" At this point in an introductory course, actors often move toward A and away from B with feigned motivation at best, and with confusion at worst.

Variation: Urgency Scale

To introduce students to urgency and commitment, I call the company to a freeze in neutral. "Good, this is exactly where you should be," I assure them. I explain that when we play games, we must play them fully committed, or at a "ten." To achieve a ten, we must adjust our urgency; no one felt a *need* to complete their goal and therefore could not fully commit to it. I explain that we'll work with an urgency scale from one to ten, where one is complete leisure and ten is a life or death situation. I instruct the company to continue to work with the same given circumstance called moments before (moving close to Person A and away from Person B), but that I will adjust them through the urgency scale as a group.

I prefer to keep this urgency scale in emotional relationship terms, rather than through vocabulary around movement or tempo. When calling the company through the scale, I also tend to skip from one-three-five-seven-eight-nine-ten, placing context around each number as I go. Individual instructors can assign relevant emotional content depending on the age and energy of the ensemble playing, but here is an example:

One: Person A is someone you were casually friendly with in high school and Person B is an old roommate to whom you owe $5.00.
Three: Person A is a good friend from high school and Person B used to cheat off of your exams and almost got you in trouble.
Five: Person A is your closest friend and Person B cheated with your spouse.
Seven: Person A is your closest friend who is currently taking self-defense classes; Person B is following you a little too closely down a dark alley.
Eight: Person A is your closest friend and he or she has a fair amount of defensive training; Person B is very likely holding a weapon and moving quite quickly.
Nine: Person A is the strongest, toughest person you know, with full defensive training; Person B definitely has a weapon and is picking up speed, fast.
Ten: Person A is the strongest person you know and can call for immediate back up; Person B is running, weapon in hand, at a breakneck speed behind you.

Once the ensemble is truly playing at a "ten," I call a freeze to neutral. In rare occurrences, I will stop an ensemble and reassert the challenge if I feel that they have not committed enough. Typically, there are just a couple of students who need some extra motivation. I'll often freeze the entire ensemble and playfully call out: "Adam, I know you could run faster than that if your life depended on it!" However, this technique is up to the style and personality of the instructor.

Once the company has completed the urgency scale and is standing at a neutral freeze, they will likely be both winded and exhilarated. Giving the ensemble a moment to catch their breath, I explain that, no matter the given circumstances, their commitment to every game needs to be at a ten. I caution that, should their commitment slip, we will return to this game for however long is necessary. I also elucidate that commitment should extend beyond theater games and scene work; like much of theater training, it will likely bleed into life.

Now, all on the same page, we pick up the Triangle Game where we left off.

Dynamics

Now that the company is playing at a ten and has the full ensemble in consideration, I make a number of calls to establish dynamics:

"Get close to Person B and away from Person A."
"Get close to Person A and away from Person B."
"Get Person A and B as close together as possible."
"Keep Person A and B as far away from each other as possible."
"Get as close as you can to both Person A and B."
"Move as far away as you can from both Person A and B."

There are, undoubtedly, many other calls that can be made to establish dynamics. As long as students focus on their objective (where/near whom they need to be) according to their relationships (Person A/B), any call is suitable. As with objective work in the Relationships section, I am able to trace Stanislavksian actions and tactics back to this portion of the game.

This leg of the exercise is also where students may laugh the most. The game is fun (and it should be—we are playing, after all!), and students enjoy how the room chaotically shifts in response to a call. As the dynamics of the space change, new stories form. Students can sense this and often impulsively graft their own narratives onto a dynamic as members chase toward and away from one another: a love triangle, a mob, a teen idol, etc. I often refer to these moments as the semester moves into improvisation or devising as a way to remind students of the intuitive nature of story making. This portion ends at the judgment of the instructor, who calls the ensemble to a neutral freeze before moving into the final leg of the game.

Triangle

Now that the ensemble is scattered throughout the space, the instructor makes the final call: the game ends when every ensemble member has created an equidistant triangle with their Person A and

B. Once every member of the company has completed this goal, the ensemble will naturally freeze, as there will be no additional need for movement. In other words, the conclusion of the game rests completely in the hands of the ensemble. I remind the company that this is a *nonverbal* game, and that there can be no gestures to make up for the lack of voice. The company must learn to listen to each other in a new way.

Here, ensemble members grapple with counterintuitive tasks: the game ends when each individual accomplishes his or her goal, but every attempt to accomplish an individual's mission affects everyone around them. As one individual moves to complete her triangle, she ruins a different triangle for another student who relies on her as a corner to his triangle. This, of course, is a great metaphor for theater and scene work: we must pursue our objectives with full commitment, but we cannot do so at the expense of our scene partners.

I will typically stop the ensemble and point out that their own goals must take into account the needs of others; that every step they take affects someone else twofold. Reacquainted with their ensemble, the company moves with more consideration. Slowly (this may take a few minutes or the remainder of the class period), and with full commitment, the ensemble solves the puzzle and finds its way into a natural freeze. I ask students to point to their As and Bs and, if I deem the game successful, congratulate the group and grant them a few minutes to chat with their triangle corners. I find that students, especially those in their first theater class, are surprised by how connected they feel to their randomly chosen partners.

At its shortest, this game will take up at least fifteen to twenty minutes. At its longest, this game can last up to an hour or more. It is at the discretion of the instructor which areas that he or she would like to lengthen, elaborate, or subtract altogether.

Conclusion

This game not only introduces skills in commitment, impulse, and ensemble work, but it acts as a point of departure for the work in the semester ahead. As noted, I often refer back to this game in a variety of units. In improvisation, I remind students that their ability to dive headfirst into relationship dynamics and recognize stories will serve them well. When approaching the Stanislavski system, performers already have a corporeal sense of objective, obstacle, and action. As we rotate into scene work, actors are reminded that they must remain conscious of their scene partner to successfully engage the text.

This game is, ultimately, an apt metaphor for the performer. It invites play and demands commitment. It utilizes movement and breath to tell a story. It showcases a range of relationships and dynamics. It emphasizes that a company is an ensemble of individuals, and that every individual piece of the puzzle is necessary to the success of the whole.

Works Cited

Applebaum, Susan. *In the Studio with Joyce Piven: Theatre Games, Story Theatre, and Text Work for Actors.* London: Methuen Drama, 2012. Print.

Evans, Mark. *Jacques Copeau.* London: Routledge, 2006. Print.

Piven, Joyce. Skype interview. 19 Aug. 2014.

Casting a Ten-Minute Play Festival or Which Way to the Acting Pool?

By Bara Swain

While I waited for my indulgent latte and lightly toasted lemon poppy muffin at the Bagel Pub in Brooklyn, I observed a young man at a nearby table studying a yellow-highlighted script. True to my nature, I approached him and asked, "What are you reading?" The surprised customer responded, "A script for class." (Oh, such a beautiful baritone!) I insisted on engaging. "So, you're an actor?" "Yes," he replied. "I'm training at Primary Stages." I nodded in approval before formally introducing myself. (Due to my tendency to ramble, I'll paraphrase.) "I'm Bara Swain, the Creative Consultant at Urban Stages in Manhattan. I produce our ten-minute play festivals. I might have casting opportunities for you in the future. Can you send me your headshot and resume?" My potential leading man's charming grin was affirmative. Or was he simply amused by my unorthodox approach? "Here's my business card," I said, fighting off that familiar imposter feeling. "I'm legit," I added brightly, "and a playwright, too!" I licked the foam off my four dollar purchase and flashed a convincing smile which, I'm told, is one of my best features.

Although I am primarily a dramatist, I have had the opportunity to cast more than 600 roles in over 225 short plays through my former employment as the Playwriting Outreach Coordinator at Abingdon Theatre Company and my present position as Creative Consultant at Urban Stages, both not-for-profit Off-Broadway theatres located six blocks from each other. At Abingdon, I co-produced the BENEFIT CHALLENGE SERIES OF TEN-MINUTE PLAYS with Literary Manager Kim T. Sharp. At Urban Stages, a vibrant theater company founded by current Artistic Director Frances Hill, my objective is to increase opportunities for diverse theater artists to participate in the creative journey of realizing new theatrical work and to make these works available to all. To date, I have produced five series of shorts for "Urban Stages New Pages," an expansion of their wide-ranging development program. At both Abingdon and Urban Stages, these ten-minute play initiatives have given playwrights the opportunity to hone their writing skills, artistic and managing directors to expand their audience base, and stage directors and actors to practice their craft and, perhaps, most importantly, to develop relationships with emerging and seasoned theater artists.

How do I cast actors? And where do I find my acting pool? Am I looking for a physical type or a particular tone or extensive training? How important is a resume in the casting process? And how does performing in a ten-minute play serve the actor? Is there an impact on the actor's future career?

Eight hours after my encounter with Brendan, I returned to my East Village digs and checked my inbox. True to his word, Brendan sent me an 8x10 glossy and a resume. I studied his credits before acknowledging receipt. Several items stood out: he was a certified phlebotomist, and he played Malcolm in the Gallery Players' production of *Macbeth*. I wrote, "Great meeting you, too, Brendan. I saw that Gallery production... I believe, five years ago!" He shot back, "Small, small world. Glad I decided to get a bagel this morning."

THE JANUARY PLAYS   *Photo by Kim T. Sharp*

Brendan's attachments were saved in my acting pool file, home of potential performing artists whom I've seen on stage, met offstage, or were recommended by colleagues. Sometimes it takes me a week to cast these actors; others, several years. In fact, the same theater that featured Brendan in Shakespeare's shortest tragedy was where I first observed the acting chops of Valerie Terranova in 2013 at their 16th Annual Black Box Festival. Valerie was cast in a short drama, Lily Rusek's *Outpost*, an expanded version of a staged reading I co-produced at Abingdon for THE SANCTUARY PLAYS. And although Valerie's physical and emotional life onstage made a deep impression on me, I did not work with her until last year when I cast her at Urban Stages in Larry Rinkel's *No Person Except* for THE PRESIDENT PLAYS. This past winter, I approached Valerie again to play a role in Daniel Damiano's *The Lepers* for THE JANUARY PLAYS. Her performance impressed me greatly.

Let's rewind. What attracted me to Brendan in the first place? Truth be told, my pool of leading young men and ingénues are, well, maturing. The actress who portrayed a 15-year old in THE COLD CASE PLAYS just became a mother; the 12-year old actress in THE CAR

THE CAR PLAYS   *Photo by Kim T. Sharp*

PLAYS is now a college sophomore; my favorite character actor who played an 18-year-old virgin in 2010 developed a receding hairline. In addition to Brendan's youth and interest in developing his craft, he followed directions (translation: he won't be late to rehearsals); he exhibited enthusiasm and eagerness to work (translation: he'll be prepared for rehearsal); and he was well-mannered (translation: he will not be combative or disrespectful toward the creative team). I also pegged him as someone who would move a set piece without complaining, instead of quoting union regulations. I hope my impression of this young man will be tested soon on stage.

Valerie Terranova
Photo by Jordan Matter

Meanwhile, Valerie Terranova continues to be on my radar. In addition to practicing her craft, what has the ten-minute play venue contributed to her career? In THE PRESIDENT PLAYS, her work was exposed to six playwrights and six directors, including celebrated Off-Broadway director Alex Dmitriev; Joan Kane, Co-Artistic Director of Ego Actus; and Aliza Shane, Artistic Director of 3 Voices Theatre. In May, Valerie performed a role in THE SLOGAN PLAYS. The two-hander, entitled *Can You Hear Me Now*, was written by—drum roll, please—yours truly! I intend to work with her again and again and again. In fact, Valerie has joined a small pool of actors who serve as my personal muse.

Enter Jessica Vera. I met my first muse in July 2008 at the Ten Grand Productions' Instant Theatre Festival. I participated as a playwright and Jessica was featured in another cast playing the crowd-pleasing title role, Dr. Bedbug. At the end of the short festival run, I approached the fearless character actress with a card that read: "I loved your performance. I look forward to seeing you grace the stage in a moment-to-moment piece." The actress dug into her pocket and retrieved a similar envelope and handed it to me. She wrote: "I admire your writing. I'd love to work with you in the future."

Jessica Vera
Photo by Douglas Gorenstein

Let's fast forward. Since our first introduction, Jessica inspired me to write *Give and Take* for THE CAR PLAYS at Abingdon. During the rehearsal process, I learned that the versatile actress is also an astute dramaturg, and her insightful comments were integral to tightening my script. To date, I have cast the sought-after actress in more than 15 short play festivals, including three plays of my own. She also joined the 36th Street Writers Block (formerly Abingdon's Playwrights Group), where her cold readings and critiques are highly valued by our playwright membership. So how has Jessica benefited since my first exposure to her work nine years ago on East 27th Street? Jessica has participated in the development process of hundreds of short and full-length plays by our extended playwriting community, and worked with dozens of stage directors in the ten-minute play genre. As a result, she has been cast in countless staged readings and productions in the metropolitan area, from the Hudson Guild Theater to the American Globe to Oberon Theater Ensemble. While many of you might say that this was the outcome of the networking process, I beg to differ. For me and many of my colleagues, we have a mutual investment in this performing artist, a professional woman with boundless energy, integrity, and intelligence, who realizes our words and contributes wholeheartedly to the process. Jessica continues to be my muse. After performing in two New York showcases of our first collaboration, *Give and Take* was selected for production at the Salem Theatre Company that same summer.

Enter Danielle Bourgeois, a spitfire of an actress with excellent instincts and stage presence. Danielle portrayed young Tacy with unbridled passion and honesty. After the second performance, I dawdled in front of the theater, sweating bullets in the Massachusetts heat, wondering if I could manage the mile-long walk back to my bed and breakfast without developing sunstroke. Suddenly, I spied pint-sized Danielle heading toward her car. I approached her for a lift.

Danielle Bourgeois
Photo by Larry Hamilton

The rest, as they say, is history. During the ride, Danielle shared her intention to move to the Big Apple. I gave her my phone number and said, "I have an extra bedroom. You're welcome to stay with me for a night or so while you look for a rental." In fact, Danielle stayed with me for three months. I introduced her to my theater community via a small role that I wrote for THE MORAL DILEMMA COMEDIES, and then THE GOSSIP PLAYS, and then our S.W.A.N. DAY festival of short plays. Today—and I just validated this fact—Danielle and I share

S.W.A.N. DAY PLAYS   *Photo by Kim. T. Sharp*

Casting a Ten-Minute Play Festival

96 mutual friends. Ninety-six mutual friends during our six-year relationship that began with an exceptional performance and a small act of kindness.

So what have you learned so far about the casting process? I'll age myself and illustrate with three proverbs:
1) Luck occurs when opportunity knocks and you answer.
2) You catch more flies with honey than vinegar.
3) Chance favors those in motion.

We've established that Danielle, Valerie, and Jessica entered my life in, well, different ways. Where did I find the other actors whom I've cast in the ten-minute play venue? Emily read stage directions before being offered a role in THE LAST RESORT PLAYS. James and I became acquainted on a bathroom line during a theater intermission prior to casting him in THE GOSSIP PLAYS. Doug was a reader for a playwriting class at HB Studio before he graced the stage in THE HOTEL PLAYS. I saw Elly in several college productions at my daughter's alma mater before bumping into her in the subway and writing a role for her in THE DENIAL PLAYS. I cast Maria from an in-house audition. She stuffed envelopes for our annual appeal before appearing in THE PRESIDENT PLAYS. Her friend Rachael attended the performance. After a cold reading in my living room, I cast Rachael

THE LAST RESORT PLAYS *Photo by Kim. T. Sharp*

in THE JANUARY PLAYS. Manini was walking her dog in my hood, Glenn was a romantic interest three decades ago, Tonia attended the same Christmas party at my neighbor's home. It goes on and on.

For these actors, did their resumes play any role (no pun intended) in the casting process? No. For me, a resume serves as a point of reference: I glance at the training and theater experience to see if we have a common factor, e.g., a particular playwright, acting teacher, venue, special skill. While some of the performers have, undoubtedly, slimmer credits than others, their experience does not affect my decision. The short play festival is an opportunity for all actors to practice their craft, from my development intern Scott Davis, an undergraduate theater major at Pace, to Carole Monferdini, a professional actress with Broadway, Off-Broadway, and extensive regional theater credits. In fact, I cast Scott as Carole's student in Abingdon's ONE-ACT NEW PLAY FESTIVAL six years ago. It was a win-win situation. Scott performed opposite an accomplished actress, and Carole exercised her acting muscles. We all had fun and, to our delight, the dramatist walked away with an award for Best Play.

Let's pause for a moment and reflect. What happened to Scott after his internship ended at Abingdon and he finished his degree? First of all, he changed his performing arts major and graduated with honors from Pace's Directing Program. In addition to numerous university directing credits, he served as assistant director for the Off-Broadway production of Songbird at 59E59 and TW 1982 at Walkerspace Theater. Since then, Scott directed at TACT, Nuyorican Poets Café, Fresh Fruit Festival, and Studio Theatre, among others. He is currently the Artistic Associate at Playhouse Creatures Theatre Company.

So, that brings us to another question that deserves a bullet.

- Why perform in a ten-minute play festival?

Many theater artists play multiple roles in their theatrical pursuits, opening up casting opportunities. For me, this certainly rings true. Casting, producing, and directing are natural extensions of my own experiences as a playwright and former actress. Creative artists participating in ten-minute play festivals often serve in other capacities. There's Brandi, a triple-threat who graced our stage several times. She serves as the artistic director of Squeaky Bicycle Productions, now in residence at Theatre for the New City. Michole, who joined us at Urban for the 36-HOUR FESTIVAL, is the artistic director of Project Y. Michael is the associate director at Metropolitan Playhouse. Charlene is the festival director of the Warner International Playwrights Festival and producing director of the Tennessee Williams Theater Festival in Provincetown. And my former house-mate, Danielle, is the co-artistic director of The Poet Acts, Inc.

Casting opportunities can also arise from the audience. Playwrights frequent these festivals in large numbers, as well as theater artists who want to support their friends and colleagues. I've seated the artistic directors from Athena Theatre and Liberation Theatre Company, high-profile and active members of theatre unions, organizations, and workshops, and, yes, the recipient of a Pulitzer Prize for Drama. In fact, a friend and colleague of mine, Doug DeVita, attended THE JANUARY PLAYS this past winter. He e-mailed me the following day for the contact information for Eric, who played opposite Valerie

The Gruesomely Merry Adventures of Nell Dash   Photo by Dennis Corsi

in Damiano's two-hander. I can't tell you how proud I was when I attended a recent production of Doug's meta-theatrical comedy, *The Gruesomely Merry Adventures of Nell Dash*. The cast featured Jessica in the title role, Doug, Carole, and Eric. And it was powerfully directed by Dennis Corsi, another festival participant. Talk about six degrees of separation! I was thrilled, and added several names to my acting pool.

Indeed, as my pool of actors, directors, and playwrights expands, so does my exposure to other theater artists. Throughout the year, I attend numerous readings and productions to support my colleagues and identify fresh talent. Josh was cast after his performance at The Network, Barbara was discovered at a Nora's Playhouse reading, Kate was my find at the T. Schreiber Shorts, and Lori hailed from a successful Nylon Fusion Theatre Company event. As a playwright, I also cast from theater companies who have produced my own work: Barrow Group, Urban Stages, Primary Stages, Articulate, Rising Sun, Ego Actus, American Globe, Kaufmann, Core Ensemble, F.A.C.T., and Bechdel Group.

Desirable Qualities of an Actor

In closing, this is what I look for when I'm casting a short play festival: an individual with talent, integrity, and a positive attitude. I seek actors who are collegial, reliable, positive, and talented. I prefer actors who respect the text and the process. And while a resume is a great tool, it is not a major factor for me.

Conclusion: Suggested Activities for Actors

What does an actor do to get cast in a festival? These are a few things that will improve your chances:

<u>Support your friends.</u> I've cast quite a few roles on the recommendation of the actors with whom I work. If I'm not familiar with their skills, I browse their websites to determine tone and type. (If you don't have a website, you might consider developing one sooner rather than later!) My rule of thumb, though, is this: If an actor

endorses another actor, I cast them in the same play. That raises the stakes for both participants.

Join a playwriting group. There are many workshops who are seeking readers for their group. If you are invited to participate, make sure that you are prompt and abide by the rules set by the group. You won't be asked back if you are disruptive or unfriendly.

Attend plays by companies that you are interested in working with. And do your homework first! Find out the names of the Artistic Director and Literary Manager. Google the director and the playwright. Perhaps you share a common interest or background. Maybe you've attended a production of theirs at another venue. If you have something good to say, approach the artist or staff member and share your thoughts. Be genuine. Flattery for flattery's sake won't get you anywhere. Follow up with a thank you note or an e-mail.

Offer your services other than acting. Are you a beginning actor? Do you want to become a member of a theater community? Offer to read stage directions, usher, help with concessions. Visit the administrative office. If there's a "Do Not Enter" sign on the door, send an e-mail. Otherwise, knock. Introduce yourself. Bring a picture that looks like you and a resume that is authentic.

Keep up your correspondence. After your final curtain call, stay in touch! I want to know whether you're interested in working with me again. Keep me informed about upcoming workshops or productions. If the time and location is feasible, I'll be there!

My life is made richer by many theater artists, on stage and off. And I'm looking forward to meeting more of you, on-stage and off. Perhaps I'll see you at my Wednesday morning stomping ground in Brooklyn… if you happen to get the urge for a bagel.

HISTORICAL DOCUMENT

Joseph Jefferson III (1829—1905), one of the most beloved actors of the nineteenth century, was on the stage from the age of four. He early established a reputation for comic playing, but Rip van Winkle was to be the mainstay of his repertory after 1865. Noted for ease, expressive action, and inventive byplay, he mingled pathos and humor in a unique combination (Brockett 414).

Rip Van Winkle was originally written by Washington Irving in 1819 and it was adapted by several playwrights. But the best version, with the help of Dion Boucicault, was by Joseph Jefferson III. Several small changes were made to the play during the forty-six years Jefferson performed it. "Between 1859 and 1905 Jefferson played Rip in literally thousands of performances. The play tells the story of an old Dutchman in the Catskill Mountains who goes to sleep and wakes up years later, and the story contains as many elements of romantic melodrama as of comedy" (Smiley 258).

Excerpts from *The Autobiography of Joseph Jefferson*, originally published in 1889

Photo by L.C. Handy Studio, Washington D.C.

Acting has been so much a part of my life that my autobiography could scarcely be written without jotting down my reflections upon it, and I merely make this little preparatory explanation to apologize for any dogmatic tone that they may possess, and to say that I present them merely as a seeker after truth in the domain of art.

In admitting the analogy that undoubtedly exists between the arts of painting, poetry, music, and acting, it should be remembered that the three former are opposed to the latter, in at least the one quality of permanence. The picture, oratorio, or book must bear the test of calculating criticism, whereas the work of an actor is fleeting: it not only dies with him, but, through his different moods, may vary from night to night. If the performance is indifferent, it is no consolation for the audience to hear that the player acted well last night, or to be told that he will act better tomorrow night; it is this night that the public has to deal with, and the impression the actor has made, good or bad, remains as such upon the mind of that particular audience.

The author, painter, or musician, if he be dissatisfied with his work, may alter and perfect it before giving it publicity, but an actor cannot rub out; he ought, therefore, in justice to his audience, to be sure of what he is going to place before it. Should a picture in an art gallery be carelessly painted we can pass on to another, or if a book fails to please us we can put it down. An escape from this kind of dullness is easily made, but in a theater the auditor is imprisoned. If the acting be indifferent, he must endure it, at least for a time. He cannot withdraw without making himself conspicuous; so he remains, hoping that there may be some improvement for the company he is in. It is this helpless condition that renders careless acting so offensive.

📖

We should act for the audience, not to the audience.

To appeal every now and then to the front of the theater for recognition is an exhibition of weakness. An actor who cannot speak a speech with his back to the audience when the situation demands it has much to learn. As soon as we acknowledge the presence of the public we dispel its attention and ruin its enjoyment. We were forced to do this in the days when we were his Majesty's servants, and when it was considered disrespectful to turn our back on royalty. How absurd to see a courtier present a document at the foot of the throne in the play and sidle up the stage with his back to the mimic king because the real article is in the royal box!

Photo by Gilbert & Bacon, Philadelphia

I have seen impulsive actors who were so confident of their power that they left all to chance. This is a dangerous course, especially when acting a new character. I will admit that there are many instances where great effects have been produced that were entirely spontaneous, and were as much a surprise to the actors who made them as they were to the audience that witnessed them; but just as individuals who have exuberant spirits are at times dreadfully depressed, so when an impulsive actor fails to receive his inspiration he is dull indeed, and is the more disappointing because of his former brilliant achievements.

In the stage-management of a play, or in the acting of a part, nothing should be left to chance, and of the reason that spontaneity, inspiration, or whatever this strange and delightful quality may be called, it is not to be commanded, or we should give it some other name. It is, therefore, better that a clear and unmistakable outline of a character should be drawn before an actor undertakes a new part. If he has a well-ordered and an artistic mind it is likely that he will give at least a symmetrical and effective performance; but should he make no definite arrangement, and depend upon our ghostly friends Spontaneity and Inspiration to pay him a visit, and should they decline to call, the actor will be in a maze and his audience will be in a muddle.

📖

Very numerous rehearsals are not always necessary to attain perfection; on the contrary, it is the quality, not the quantity, that is important. Tedious preparation day after day will sometimes pall upon a company of actors, who, wearied by constant repetition, lose the freshness with which their performance should be given; and that quality once lost is seldom regained. It is vain for a manager to argue that he pays the actor for his time and attention. He has a perfect right to these, certainly; but the feeling and enthusiasm with which the time and attention should be given he can no more command than he can alter the human nature of his company.

Just as an early impression is the most indelible, so the first rehearsal is the most important, and being so should never be called until the author and stage-manager shall have fully digested their plans and thoroughly understand what they intend to do. This course not only saves labor but begets the respect of the company, who feels that their time will not be wasted and that they are in the hands of patient and conscientious directors.

It is the time-honored excuse of some actors that they cannot study a part until they have rehearsed it, forgetting that it is not possible to rehearse properly until they are perfect in the words. A part is more easily studied after a rehearsal of it, certainly; but I am not discussing ease, remember, but propriety. How can we watch the action and progress of the play if our eyes are bent upon the book? It is merely a bad habit, and one that has grown out of a desire that some people have to shirk their duty; being naturally inclined to procrastination they shelter themselves under this weak and conventional excuse.

Usually the scenery and properties of a play are brought into requisition during the later rehearsals, and increased in detail till they culminate at the last rehearsal.

This is working from the wrong direction. It is at the first rehearsal that these adjuncts should be used, and if they are not ready substitutes should be put in their places; for if the set of the scene, the chairs, tables, and other mechanical arrangements are placed upon the stage for an initial rehearsal, the manager and the actors know then and ever afterwards where to find them and how to arrange their groupings, exits, entrances, and stage business in accordance with the position of these useful materials; but if, after all the stage business has been arranged, the company suddenly find at the last rehearsal that chairs, tables, seats, etc. are met upon the stage in unexpected places, they become obstacles to the actors instead of adjuncts.

I do not mean to say that the entire business of a play can be arranged at the first rehearsal. New ideas continually crop up during the early stages of preparation which upon consideration may be more valuable than the original ones, and actors may have suggestions to make, the effect of which had not struck the author. But while a good general shows his genius best when dealing with an emergency, he does not disdain to plan the battle before the action takes place.

Better have no rehearsal at all than one that is long, ramblings and careless: a clearly cut and perfectly defined outline gives precision and finish to the work. If it were possible the pantomime and action of a play should reveal its meaning to an audience without the aid of dialogue; this would give force to the language and enable those who do not catch all the words fully to comprehend their meaning.

Much has been written upon the question as to whether an actor ought to feel the character he acts or be dead to any sensations in this direction. Excellent artists differ in their opinions on their important point. In discussing it I must refer to some words I wrote in one of the early chapters of this book: "The methods by which actors arrive at great effects vary according to their own natures; this renders the teaching of the art by any strictly defined lines a difficult master."

There has lately been a discussion on the subject, in which many have taken part, and one quite notable debate between two distinguished actors, one of the English and the other of the French stage. These gentlemen, though they differ entirely on their ideas, are, nevertheless, equally right. The method of one, I have no doubt, is the best he could possibly devise for himself; and the same may be said of

Photo by Napoleon Sarony, New York.

the rules of the other as applied to himself. But they must work with their own tools; if they had to adopt each other's they would be as much confused as if compelled to exchange languages. One believes that he must feel the character he plays, even to the shedding of real tears, while the other prefer never to lose himself for an instant, and there is no doubt that they both act with more effect by adhering to their own dogmas.

For myself, I know that I act best when the heart is warm and the head is cool. In observing the works of great painters I find that they have no conventionalities except their own; hence they are masters, and each is at the head of his own school. They are original, and could not imitate even if they would.

So with acting, no master-hand can prescribe rules for the head of another school. If, then, I appear bold in putting forth my suggestions, I desire it to be clearly understood that I do not present them to original or experienced artists who have formed their school, but to the student who may have a temperament akin to my own, and who could, therefore, blend my methods with his preconceived ideas.

I think it is generally conceded that imitators are seldom fine actors, though they are usually great favorites with the public. I confess that I enjoy the exhibitions of this kind of talent exceedingly. There is something very attractive and even strange to see one man display the voice, manner, and expression of another- particularly if that other be not yourself. We may enjoy the imitation of our dearest friends, but our smiles vanish and our faces elongate if the mimic attempts to give " a counterfeit presentment" of the party of the first part. I have heroically tried on several occasions to enjoy imitations of myself, but have never succeeded. These ingenious transcripts contain a slight touch of ridicule that always offends the original. An anecdote of Mr. Buckstone, the English comedian, will serve to illustrate what I have said. He was an actor whose mannerisms were so marked that they infused themselves through all the characters he played. He was undoubtedly humorous, or, more properly speaking, funny; but whether he acted Sir Andrew Aguecheek or Cousin Joe he seemed to have no power of embodying the character- rendering each of them with the same voice, manner, and attitude; consequently, he was an admirable subject for imitation.

At the close of a dinner party he had been given to understand that there was a person present who gave an excellent imitation of himself. Buckstone at once desired the gentleman to let the company have a test of his quality. The gentleman politely declined, saying that he might give offense; but the comedian would not let him off, insisted on the exhibition, and, rubbing his hands together with great glee, settled himself down for unlimited enjoyment. The imitator, seeing that there was no escape, arose, and amid breathless silence began. His hit was immense, and as he sat down the guests broke forth in loud laughter and applause: the whole table was in a roar of merriment; everyone was in ecstasy except Buckstone, who looked the picture of misery.

"Well, Mr. Buckstone," exclaimed a wag, who was quietly enjoying the comedian's discomfiture, "don't you think the imitation very fine?"

"It may be," he replied, "but I think I could do it better myself."

Acting is more a gift than an art. I have seen a child impress an audience by its natural grace and magnetism. The little creature was too young to know what art meant, but it had the gift of acting. The great value of art when applied to the stage is that it enables the performer to reproduce the gift, and so move his audience night after night, even though he has acted the same character a thousand times. In fact, we cannot act a character too often, if we do not lose interest in it. But when its constant repetition palls on the actor it will surely weary his audience. When you lose interest-stop acting.

It is the freshness, the spontaneity, of acting that charms. How can a weary brain produce this quality? Show me a tired actor and I will show you a dull audience. They may go in crowds to see him, and sit patiently through his performance. They have heard that he is great, they may even know it from past experience; so they accept the indifferent art, thinking, perhaps, that they are to blame for a lack of enthusiasm.

Many instructors in the dramatic art fall into the error of teaching too much. The pupil should first be allowed to exhibit his quality, and so teach the teacher what to teach. This course would answer the double purpose of first revealing how much the pupil is capable of learning, and, what is still more important, of permitting him to display his powers untrammeled. Whereas, if the master begins by pounding his dogmas into the student, the latter becomes environed by a foreign influence which, if repugnant to his nature, may smother his ability.

Photo by Napoleon Sarony, New York.

While acting once in Boston I received a note from the publisher of "The Atlantic Monthly," to know if I would call at the publishing house to meet Mrs. Harriet Beecher Stowe. It seems the lady had been at the theater where I had acted the night before, and in a note to the publisher had expressed a desire to see me. We had a long and, to me, a very pleasant chat. In speaking of her visit to the theater she said she was struck by the scene in which Rip meets with his daughter, and that it reminded her of the situation between Lear and Cordelia. I told her that the scene was undoubtedly modeled on the one from Shakespeare, and perhaps the white hair and beard floating about the head of the old Knickerbocker had some share in this likeness. She said she was sure that I could play Lear. I was sorry to differ with a lady, but I told her I was quite sure that I could not.

Shortly after this I met another lady of equal intelligence, who seemed much interested in Rip Van Winkle. Among the many questions she asked of me was how I could at the character so often and not tire of it. I told her that I had always been strangely interested in the part, and fearing that I might eventually grow weary of it, I had of late years so arranged my seasons that I played only a few months and took long spells of rest between them, but that my great stimulus, of course, was public approval, and the knowledge that it must cease if I flagged in my interest or neglected to give my entire attention to the work while it was progressing.

"Another question, please. Why don't you have a dog in the play?"

I replied that I disliked realism in art, and realism alive, with a tail to wag at the wrong time, would be abominable.

"But don't' you think that the public would like to see Schneider?"

"The public could not pay him a higher compliment, for it shows how great an interest they take in an animal that has never been exhibited. No, no; 'hold the mirror up to nature' if you like, but don't hold nature up- a reflection of the thing, but not the thing itself. How badly would a drunken man give an exhibition of intoxication on the stage! Who shall act a madman but one who is perfectly sane? We must not be natural but appear to be so."

Works Cited

Brockett, Oscar G. *History of the Theatre*. Allyn and Bacon, 1995. Print.

Jefferson, Joseph. *The Autobiography of Joseph Jefferson*. The Century Company, 1889. Print.

Smiley, Sam. *Theatre, The Human Art*. Harper and Row, 1987. Print.

Cracking Shakespeare: A Hands-on Guide for Actors and Directors +Video
by Kelly Hunter
London: Bloomsbury Methuen Drama, 2015

Reviewed by Suzanne Delle

To write another book on Shakespeare or not, that is the question. Most academics might agree that anything worth saying about the man and his work has been said. However, Kelly Hunter's latest, *Cracking Shakespeare*, is more a manual for directors and acting teachers to assist their students in unlocking the secrets of acting Shakespeare's scripts rather than a look at history or the plays. In fact, there are very few practical handbooks for those interested in approaching Shakespeare's works for performance and not literature, and this is a welcome addition to that assemblage.

Hunter divides her book into three sections: Rhythm, Sound, and Structure; Words, Words, Words; and Games to Play in Rehearsal. Many students feel stymied by the language in the plays so Hunter explores different techniques in each section to break Shakespeare's text down into understandable ideas. She clearly states that her goal in the writing of the book is to help actors make the language feel like it's their own. Focusing on verse speaking, the book starts with iambic pentameter and how it is used to express the emotions of the character. While some of the exercises may remind the reader of their high school English class (like the pages on alliteration and scansion), she approaches all of the exercises from the emotional through-line perspective of the character. This culminates in the final chapters, which focus on soliloquies and scene work.

Hunter doesn't just concentrate on the word however; she includes physical exercises to help ensure that the actor is clear on meaning and subtext. In fact, most of these exercises could be used in rehearsals for contemporary plays as well to help young actors bring their work more into their body.

While Hunter focuses on Hamlet's first soliloquy ("O that this too too solid flesh would melt" 1. 2), she also uses examples from many plays including *King Lear*, *Macbeth*, *All's Well That Ends Well*, *Twelfth Night* and others. What this means is that the better read one is of the canon, the more the reader will understand the point of the exercises in *Cracking Shakespeare* and not have to take the extra step to learn about plot before exploring the emotional alphabet or rhetoric. Since the intended audience for the book is probably teachers and directors, that may not be a hindrance to understanding for most. But if a young actor picks up this book, she may find the multitude of examples off-putting.

Hunter is herself an actor and director of Shakespeare's plays, having worked with the Royal Shakespeare Company, British American Drama Academy, and the Royal Central School of Speech and Drama. This experience has led her to develop many of the exercises outlined in the book and has allowed her access to students in order to film herself working on the techniques with them. The accompanying videos are a great companion to the book especially in today's classroom where students have grown up with technology and many are visual learners. Also in many acting classes, students are taught by watching others and responding to their classmates' work; therefore, the accompanying videos can be used to model the exercises before they are tried out on actors. The videos are all online, as opposed to a CD, and can be accessed by both student and director from any device. As students watch actors in the videos struggle with the exercises and ask questions, it will help them overcome their own fears of looking foolish as they try the breath or scaffolding exercises in front of their peers.

This book will be helpful for anyone who teaches classical acting. Even if you already have techniques and activities that are tried and true, Hunter's exercises will be a welcome addition to your classroom. Start at the beginning and build a course around them or pick and choose from them, depending on a specific problem found during rehearsal. *Cracking Shakespeare* is a detailed how-to book for one of the more frightening aspects of theatrical training: the Shakespearean text. It is a welcome addition to the field of acting training and fills a void left by so many books that focus solely on contemporary (Stanislavski) acting.

Performing in Comedy: A Student's Guide
by Ian Angus Wilkie
London: Routledge, 2016

Reviewed by Matt Fotis

While comic performance is often either casually dismissed or described through vague notions of comedic timing, Ian Wilkie's *Performing in Comedy* is built on the premise that acting in comedy is a distinct art form that requires specific skills and rigorous training. Mixing theoretical underpinnings of comedy with practical exercises, Wilkie guides the reader through a variety of comic styles, theories, and skills. Examples and suggestions for additional resources abound, making this text a needed addition for acting students and teachers.

Given that comic performance is so dependent on the connection between performer and audience, Wilkie builds his study around the concept of the actor as a "reflective-practitioner." This concept focuses on the importance for the actor to continuously assess and reflect on his or her performance, the relationship with co-performers and audience, and the comic text itself. According to Wilkie, this reflective approach "will keep the comedy that you co-create fresh, fully informed and valuably reimagined for each and every performance" (198). There are numerous examples and exercises throughout to help develop reflective skills, including several "reflective checklist" questions in the appendix aimed at "employing Stanislavskian ways to create 'character from within' while also using Brechtian methods to directly affect the audience" (202). Wilkie's goal is to create a comic performer who uses the character-building tools of Stanislavski, while selectively applying Brechtian techniques to connect with the audience and actively assess and reflect on his or her own performance.

Within the framework of the "reflective-practitioner," Wilkie organizes the book around several key skills needed to be an effective comic performer: interplay with the audience; interplay with the ensemble; rhythm and timing; finding comic truthfulness; and the comic text itself. The book begins by providing a theoretical framework for comedy, including a brief overview of the three major philosophies of humor: relief, superiority, and incongruity. One of the book's great pedagogic strengths is how Wilkie weaves comic theory throughout to contextualize and deepen the practical skills explored. Each chapter also ends with suggestions for further reading, often pointing the reader to historical or theoretical works.

In chapter 2, Wilkie examines the relationship between the performer and the audience. He explores the audience's connection to the comedic performance, specifically looking at how the performer can analyze the "quality of their laughter" (25), and ascertains that in order for the performance to be effective, the laughs "must be gained appropriately" (38). Wilkie argues that the performer's relationship with the audience is rooted in the performer's ability to make his or her character multi-dimensional and likeable. "The performer has to radiate some humanity, often despite of and through the stereotype that is represented" (28). For Wilkie, likeability is often found by the performer displaying the character's vulnerability, which will allow the audience the opportunity to relate to and empathize with even the most inherently dislikeable character. The chapter concludes with a brief analysis of comic audiences themselves and the communal aspects of laughter.

Chapter 3 analyzes the interplay between performers, as well as the idea of comic truthfulness. This chapter is loaded with ensemble-building exercises. While the exercises themselves are not particularly groundbreaking, the emphasis on the reliance between performers is examined in light of ensemble storytelling. While many exercises and books focus on the individual performer, Wilkie makes it a point to emphasize the role of the entire ensemble in creating comedy. Within this concept of ensemble, Wilkie examines the concept of comic truthfulness, which again focuses on the quality and layers of laughter, and is linked to accessing and portraying a character's vulnerability—both by an individual actor and the ensemble as a whole. Throughout the book, Wilkie extols the virtue of truthful performance and includes several exercises aimed at finding and playing the truth within a character.

Rhythm and timing, the most nebulous of comic skills, are the topics of chapter 4. Rather than relying on a performer's natural timing, Wilkie breaks down the timing and rhythm of several popular comic texts, from knock-knock jokes to Shakespeare's fools. The chapter itself is roughly split into two categories: verbal and physical timing. Wilkie spends a good deal of the chapter looking at the rhythm of a text, including an analysis of accents and dialects as clues and cues to a performer. Several traditional wordplay exercises are included to help reinforce and develop verbal timing for performers. Perhaps understandably, the physical timing section is less detailed than the verbal section, though Wilkie does provide a small treatise on the humor inherent in slipping on a banana peel to help illustrate the theoretical base of physical humor.

While Wilkie acknowledges the extent to which comedy is reliant upon performance, chapter 5 provides textual analysis tools for working with comic texts. This chapter strays farthest into theoretical and historical territory, enumerating the historical sources for Western comic writing and tying classical comic tropes to contemporary comic expression. Wilkie devotes a large segment of the chapter to linking "the text" to the previously discussed comic skills (such as interplay, rhythm, truthfulness). He illustrates how to find in texts the three comic principles—relief, superiority, and incongruity—and how to use them. He likewise spends a good deal of this chapter on the interplay inherent in many comic texts, as well as discovering the truth and vulnerability in comic characters via textual clues.

Chapter 6 tackles comic acting in film and television, but primarily describes the differences between theater and film, while the exercises often center on those differences (e.g., properly sizing your performance for the screen rather than the stage) rather than on specific comic skills. Chapter 7 is a sampling of various interviews and quotations from comic performers that highlight and reinforce the principal ideas of the book. Chapter 8, "The Happy Ending," provides a concise and highly effective recap of the book's main concepts and how they relate to the concept of the "reflective-practitioner" that is woven throughout the book. Written with a commendable blend of theory and practice, *Performing in Comedy* provides a broadly-based and highly effective approach to comic acting. With a myriad of traditional and new exercises, as well as a list for further reading and research attached to the end of each chapter, Wilkie provides a solid foundation not only for the aspiring performer, but also for further inquiry into comic performance. While the examples used throughout are heavily weighted toward British television and performance, Wilkie provides the reader with a quick guide to access the material to augment the chapters. *Performing in Comedy* is an equally effective theoretical primer and practical handbook.

Actor Movement: Expression of the Physical Being
by Vanessa Ewan and Debbie Green
London: Bloomsbury Press, 2015

Reviewed by Jenn Ariadne Calvano

In *Actor Movement: Expression of the Physical Being*, Vanessa Ewan and Debbie Green integrate aspects and concepts from a myriad of movement-based training approaches with their own training pedagogy in the three-year acting course at the Royal Central School of Speech and Drama. Their book aims to offer "elements of the thinking and practice of a live example of a three-year progression of movement for acting" (xii), through explaining the philosophy behind its movement work and well as providing examples and exercises for training.

The book is made up of nine chapters. Beginning with a general introduction, the structure of the book reflects a progression of a movement-based actor training program, establishing a foundation through awareness building, neutral work, and action and image, respectively, in chapters two, three, and four. Building on these skills, chapters five, six, and seven address observation and analysis, physical work with animal and anthropomorphic lenses, and expressive, emotional journey. The book concludes with advanced Laban work and safety in chapters eight and nine.

In introducing the book, the authors list a wide prospective audience of actors and students interested in expressive movement as well as theater teachers and creators doing movement work. Each chapter begins with an overview, continues to articulate the authors' approach to movement, and concludes with detailed practical exercises. A truly disciplined actor may enjoy reading through the entire philosophy section once to give her context before reading through a second time and flipping back and forth between the philosophy section to the corresponding exercises at the end of the chapter, and in some cases in the appendix. On the other hand, this structure makes for an awkward flow for the actor who wants to work straight through the book. A smattering of video link symbols can be found throughout the book. At the end of the book is a list of the 26 exercises that have corresponding video links on a Vimeo webpage. These supplement the written "in context" practical application instructions for a handful of the exercises listed throughout the book, giving "visual insight into the experience of an exercise or a process outlined in the text." However, there is no explanation or clear reasoning why some exercises receive video demonstration rather than others or all of them.

As a movement instructor, I found the exercises very useful, especially in building upon and expanding the underpinning philosophy, which is articulated particularly well for those with a strong movement background. However, these exercises might be less accessible to the actor with little training or training only in a single approach to movement. The authors use vocabulary, concepts, and exercises that include elements of Laban, Lecoq, Copeau, Alexander, Feldenkrais, Grotowski, and other approaches. While the unpacking of concepts such as *neutral* in chapter 3 and *observation* in chapter 5 are enlightening and quite useful for those at any point of their actor training, someone with extensive movement training will be better equipped to follow instructions such as "keep the hip joint released" (44), "transfer the essence" (114), or "rebalance his awareness" (134). Additionally, key points such as "a large element of this is not about doing; it's about handing over to the work you have already done" (170) could be more easily processed by a novice actor with the aid of a fellow performer, director, or instructor. Although the second chapter of the book focuses on *connecting with the body*, this book alone cannot replace the guidance of a movement instructor for beginners.

I admire the book's emphasis on process over product, but this is a potentially tough focus for the student to absorb without an instructor to help. Perhaps the book's greatest pedagogical value is as a supplemental resource, but it may also usefully serve as a challenge to an instructor's established approach to movement. Movement instructors additionally will find inspiration from its contextual explanations of movement work as well as a myriad of exercises that can be adapted to supplement or evolve a current approach.

Roadblocks in Acting
by Rob Roznowski
London: Palgrave, 2017

Reviewed by Dennis Schebetta

In *Roadblocks in Acting*, Roznowski has created a self-described "self-help" book to aid actors, directors, and teachers navigate the psychological rigors of the craft. Although actors receive training in technique, they rarely learn strategies on how to engage in emotionally high-charged imaginary circumstances in a healthy way, and instructors are often unconcerned or unequipped with tools to assist or nurture mental and psychological well-being. The book's goal is to use standardized assessments and practical exercises to identify, address, and overcome roadblocks, what Roznowski identifies as "self-imposed barriers to holistic embodied acting on stage or on camera" (1) so that actors can reach "peak performance" in a healthy way. These roadblocks are not skill-based or physical-based techniques, but an "emotionally triggered hindrance" that inhibits the freedom of the actor's work (2). In particular, the book's aim is to address actors who play it safe by making the same choices over and over again, or avoid emotionally charged material, or feel they are holding themselves back in some mysterious way. However, the book delivers much more than its promise, providing an insightful, well-researched overview of the psychological aspects of the profession. In addition, it could even serve as a much-needed guidebook on ethics in the classroom, giving students and educators the knowledge and tools to understand the psychological dimensions of actor training.

Roznowski draws on his many years of experience teaching as Associate Professor and Head of Acting and Directing at Michigan State University. Like many professors, he observed highly-skilled students struggling to achieve artistic excellence and finding freedom in their work, not because of training or effort, but some other unknown block (1). Roznowski enlisted the aid of four psychologists to help him to identify and address these blocks in an effort to create a "bridge" (2) to overcome them. These four psychologists were familiar with acting and its relation to psychology, neuroscience, and cognitive science. Roznowski explored these ideas with over a hundred graduate and undergraduate students. In addition to transcripts and quotes from these sources, Roznowski refers to a range of research and recent studies, such as those by Rhonda Blair (*The Actor, Image, and Acting: Acting and Cognitive Neuroscience*) and Rick Kemp (*Embodied Acting: What Neuroscience Tells Us About Performance*), plus examples from *The Australian Actors' Wellbeing Study* conducted by doctors working with the Australian actors union. Going beyond theory and scientific data, Roznowski has successfully clarified these ideas for the layperson and applied them to hands-on exercises. For example, he modifies Mel Shapiro's well-known autodrama exercise and applies that to his concepts, effectively theatricalizing the roadblock to investigate it and thus become free of it. Another helpful tool borrowed from the expert consultants is the use of third-person writing and self-talk within the audition and rehearsal process, as well as in performance, to create emotional safety and to reduce anxiety. The book is geared toward actors who have acquired technique and have already begun working on their craft, as well as their directors, coaches, and teachers, although beginning actors could also benefit.

The introduction and first chapter define the term roadblock and how each is a unique personal issue. They also address the dynamics of the unspoken power structures of an acting class. In particular, there is a detailed example from an actor struggling with an emotional moment in a production, with commentary from both actor and director, as well as the psychological reasons that particular roadblock may have manifested. Roznowski asserts immediately and throughout the book that acting should not be used in place of therapy, and that acting teachers are not therapists, mentioning when professional assistance might be necessary. Chapter 2, "Understanding Your Self," introduces concepts from neuroscience and psychology, providing self-analysis exercises. Actors analyze their emotional or psychological reasons for choosing the profession, and then identify how this might influence certain choices, especially if those choices are habits of safety that limit potential. Roznowski treads some uneasy territory here, at one level proclaiming that "each person's journey is unique" (25), so the reasons for which an actor chooses the profession can vary. But he also posits that there are two primary psychological motives to fill an "emotional void"—either "they like attention" or "they do it lose their self, to hide" (25). Roznowski admits this is a reductionist oversimplification, but the categories allow for quick identification of an actor's approach. If, as an actor, you disagree with the statement, you may well have issues with his further arguments about the personal and professional overlap of the actor's work. However, the author defuses the idea of two basic needs for pursuing acting by relating his own reluctance to diminish his reasons for acting. This awareness then led to a recognition of his own need for deep honesty, realizing that the idea of fulfilling an emotional need is "not a judgment but a practical provocation to deeper examination of self related to art" (26).

The author expands further on these two classifications and emotional choices in Chapter 3, "Understanding Your Other Selves," as these psychological concepts of the self affect how actors have multiple selves: professional, personal, and character. These selves merge and overlap and the first step is to examine the personal self, using standardized assessment tests, tools from the realm of psychology such as the Big-Five and the Five Factor Model, and testing levels of introvert/extrovert. The Big-Five is a psychological personality test which examines "five broad areas or traits including extroversion, agreeableness, conscientiousness, neuroticism and openness to experience" (41). After taking the Big-Five once, the exercises then lead the actor through the various selves, taking the test as the "actor self" and as characters that he or she has played in the past. Following that, the introvert/extrovert test analyzes the actor's different selves as well. Here, Roznowski relates research that illuminates personality types who may be shy personally, and yet perform freely as actors, making choices that would otherwise belong to an extrovert. While many actors may be familiar with self-analysis or character biography exercises, these standardized tests are more specific, allowing an actor to clearly see how each self is different and juggled in various ways, consciously or unconsciously, in rehearsal, on stage, or backstage. Using scientific data, Roznowski illuminates how actors have unique stressors, with clear evidence that this work takes a toll physically, mentally, and psychologically. These stress factors can also lead to blocks in the actor's process.

The next few chapters identify various roadblocks, and then provide practical exercises to overcome them. Roznowski uses various examples from students and professional actors to show how roadblocks unveil themselves through safety behaviors which may manifest as areas of physical tension, a nervous tic, avoiding eye contact, tugging at clothes, physical discomfort, or vocal qualities. Other noticeable behaviors might include using humor to avoid intimacy or over-critical judgment. Roznowski then introduces strategies for working with this information, such as Acceptance Commitment Therapy (ACT) which is a theory of non-judgmental awareness or "a tangible way in which actors may begin to examine their work more objectively" (68). Actors become aware of an issue, accept it, and embrace it as part of that present moment. ACT "reminds you this is only a temporary state of being" (68). The author then gives concrete examples of actors working through such blocks as using intelligence to avoid empathy, a fear of looking foolish, and feeling self-conscious about height. Chapter 6, "Addressing Roadblocks," delves into a series of sequential exercises designed for both actors and acting teachers to use as methods to address blocks. Examples of these exercises are changing the tempo of a scene, exaggerating the roadblock, physicalizing or vocalizing the roadblock, inner monologue exercises, and meditation. The author expands further on manifestation of roadblocks, and deeply explains further issues including anxiety, body awareness, emotion, hiding, intimacy, judgment, power, and self-esteem. The final issue, vulnerability, is described as the "meta" roadblock, underlying all other issues. The ability to be vulnerable is described early in the book as one of three adjectives that define successful acting (the other two are *adept* and *skilled*). Roznowski defines vulnerability as "compassionate understanding of a character in combination with an empathetic ability to explore emotional territory required by the script" (5). Many actors may have their own definition so it's important that actors understand what they are striving for and why, and not push emotion for its own sake or pretend to be vulnerable even though they're not. Here, the author cautions against "too much vulnerability" (162) and states that normalizing vulnerability can be an anxiety-filled journey. According to Roznowski, success seems also to lie in "small moments of vulnerability" (165), and by scaffolding in small amounts, students can attain their desired vulnerability over time. The final two chapters emphasize the need for repetition and practice to build bridges to overcome barriers, in order both to enjoy excellence and to experience the mindfulness that results from peak performance.

The strength of this book is that it can be used individually as a self-help guide to examine one's work, but also in a classroom setting. The examples and excerpts from previous students are helpful and specific, with common issues that many students face (e.g., fear of intimacy, emotional blocks, stage fright). What is particularly helpful is that Roznowski provides many resources for the reader to learn more about the concepts and theories addressed. The author also admits that since these concepts derive from the areas of psychology and neuroscience, the strategies are particularly well suited to a Stanislavski-based training. He briefly mentions other styles of performance such as Shakespeare, musical theater, Commedia, and mask, but spends limited time detailing how to apply these exercises to other styles. He does suggest and encourage modifications, however, and provides a few examples, so it would be easy enough for a specialist in these styles to adapt the book's ideas.

This insightful and inspiring book clearly hits the mark in its aim to give tools to actors who keep making the same choices over and over again or for those who want to push themselves out of their comfort zones into highly-charged performances. For those willing to dive into the exercises honestly, it is a true actor's guide in self-discovery and self-awareness, offering useful psychological concepts to develop the actor's instrument in a healthy way. If you are an acting teacher, director, or coach, you will find it invaluable in aiding students to overcome their blocks.

A Director's Guide to Stanislavsky's Active Analysis
by James Thomas
London: Bloomsbury, 2016

&

Actioning — and How to Do It
by Nick Moseley
London: Nick Hern Books, 2016

by Leigh Woods

Different as these books are in approach, style, and instructional matter, they are similar in their commemorative projects and in the deference they pay to their Stanislavskyan heritage. James Thomas has had "nearly two decades of classes and discussions with master teachers at the Moscow Art Theatre School" as background for his book (Thomas 1), while Nick Moseley attributes the practices he calls "actioning" to the United Kingdom's Joint Stock Theatre Company under the left-leaning stewardship of William Gaskill and Max Stafford-Clark in the 1970s (Moseley vii).

Both authors credit Constantin Stanislavsky as progenitor of the ideas and practices they advocate, though Thomas is far more focused on Stanislavsky's disciple Maria Knebel, and on her own disciple Anatoly Efros (1-2) for having relayed key analytics and rehearsal practices derived from Stanislavsky himself. Both books are brief, as befits the manual each presents itself to be. Both authors have written other books and have long experience as practitioners, teachers, and administrators. Each of their approaches recommends itself for being applicable to any kind of script performed by any group of actors.

The challenge for every latter-day interpreter of the Russian master has been to determine *which* Stanislavsky offers the optimal point of entry. That decision often hinges on which of his advocates is considered to be the most faithful in relaying his notions through the disputes that have dogged his legacy, and which were unfolding even while he was living. He could be oracular in his florid way with words, to judge his accounts, as I must, from their translated or adapted versions in English.

The first half of Thomas's book offers a brisk synoptic treatment of "A Director's Work with Active Analysis," while the second half offers his translation of Maria Knebel's seminal essays about her work with the living Stanislavsky. Although the essays were published only later, between the 1950s and the early 1970s, they capture what Knebel took to be the relationship between what she and others knew as Active Analysis and the use of serial improvisations, which Stanislavsky called *études*, to help actors discover the most essential elements in characters and scenes they play.

Thomas refers readers twice to his own *Script Analysis for Actors, Directors, and Designers* for offering the most thorough account of the analytical methods he admires and applies in the form Knebel lays them out. This mode of analysis is called on to inform any *études* that may be undertaken under a director's strict supervision during rehearsals. Thomas recommends that *études* be used after only relatively brief table work, the better, he says in agreeing with Knebel, to introduce actors to the dramatic text itself and to inspire them to exercise an incremental magic that will help them bring their characters to life.

Thomas's discussions, nearly as much as Knebel's, are redolent with organic metaphors about process and about the arts in general. This derives from Stanislavsky's debt to Romanticism and the credo that any art, including plays and their stagings, will grow and evolve much as plants and animals do. The *études* themselves represent an organicism that has actors engaging the text before they have learned any of it or begun even to sound out its words. The gains for the actors are, in an ideal world, originality and a wider suggestibility.

Active Analysis can serve anyone, director, actor, or designer, and *études* might be effective when used by performers experienced at speaking classical or otherwise ornate texts. I found it hard to imagine it serving amateurs well under the supervision even of a director experienced in devising and conducting *études*. A longer rehearsal period than usual would be an advantage, as it often was for Stanislavsky himself. In professional, academic, and amateur productions, rehearsal time is always at a premium, as Thomas himself notes in his chapter on "Rehearsal Realities" (79-82). Action as prolific as it is in Shakespeare's plays, for instance, demands sustained attention to the text itself, as I think most of us would agree.

Considerable skill would be demanded of directors in finding *études* to meet the needs of the ensemble and of any text they mean to serve and enliven. It was easy for me to imagine *études* becoming an end in themselves, and they seem to have been so for Maria Knebel, who evidences a kind of rehearsal-junkie mentality. I have never found my experiences with improvisations that had us actors using our own words in place of the playwright's either satisfying or instructive. I saw it called on most often during the late 1960s and early 1970s when an ethos of anti-authoritarianism prevailed that rendered classic texts as inherently tyrannizing and which valorized any personal expression they sparked as liberated, enlightened, and genuine, or in the current word in fashion, "authentic."

Thomas's allegiance to his Soviet- and post-Soviet on-site training and mentors is strong, and what they have given him has animated his career and founded his scholarship in the Russian language and in translating documents of significance. He states that the method he espouses is not the only one that can be serviceable (xiv); but I found his initial discussion of Active Analysis too abbreviated to be easily understood or applied without help from Thomas's own *Script Analysis*. His confidence in Knebel's take on Stanislavsky, as if she had been channeling the great man after his death, seemed unquestioned. Veneration along these lines has long cropped up among acting teachers and directors in the United States, and Lee Strasberg and Stella Adler, among others, claimed greater authority for their pedagogies owing to their claim of having captured the essence of the Stanislavsky's teaching, and in Strasberg's case, translating it into an American and more filmic idiom.

I found Nick Moseley's *Actioning*, which he regards as a more recent and United-Kingdom-specific offshoot of Active Analysis, more cohesive and self-contained. It holds that individual lines make the most elemental segments that actors are called on to engage and relay, and which offer the best medium for integrating voice and body and for building urgency in a scene. Actioning evokes a kinesthetic and dynamic understanding of what acting can be at its best, and it recommends itself as a method that can be applied to a wide range of plays, canonical and otherwise.

Actioning requires actors to make the most essential decisions regarding how to play their characters by searching out a distinctive verb to apply to each line of dialogue. The first chapter, "Beginning Actioning," lays out the method by drawing examples from simple scenes. The second chapter takes up challenges that lie in more complex scripts, and the remaining six chapters implement and refine the approach. The atomizing of scripts in this manner stands to tie actors more closely to text than to subtext or exposition, as is the thrust of the *études* in Thomas's book.

In the hands of seasoned actors, actioning falls in with the physicalized approaches to verse-speaking championed over the last couple of generations by Cicely Berry and Kristin Linklater, among others. Actioning offers a more explicit way of delivering dialogue which, ideally, integrates voice and body and so keeps them in balance.

The degree to which Moseley bases actioning on textual analysis is laudable, in my opinion. So many theater students—acting majors often, but by no means they exclusively—will tend to read scripts through the eyes of whatever character they play, or with an impressionism hatched in their mind's eye. Performances shaped by reading a play more closely are to be desired and encouraged, and such work can allow a more comprehensive view of the larger enterprise and the sort of collaborations it will require. *Actioning*'s emphasis on text and the possibilities to be found there distinguishes it from Thomas's (and Knebel's) reliance on *études* improvised around the text as a preliminary channel into the play.

With that, I found Moseley's advice that actors settle on a distinctive verb for each line overdetermined and potentially dispersive of focus and energy. He views vigor as key to any actor's expressive obligation, and he asserts that vocal means will dovetail with bodily ones when a suitable verb can be found, tested, and enacted for each line spoken. Finding a different verb for every line poses a significant challenge in itself, or so I imagined it would, and Moseley mentions Marina Calderone and Maggie Lloyd-Williams' *Actions: The Actors' Thesaurus* (Nick Hern, 2004) as a supplement for enlarging actors' stores of verbs that will be necessary to apply actioning. Combing some of the less traveled corners of one's own language can feel not unlike studying a foreign one, and may also have its own ancillary benefits.

I was impressed with the arrays of verbs Moseley rolled out in his sample analyses. I also thought it would be hard for any actor to command a lexicon adequate for any complex or lengthy scene approached in this manner. Occasionally, virtually synonymous pairings pointing to dramatic progressions, like "unnerve" and "disconcert" (36), or "mock" and "outclass" (38), or "stir" and "provoke" (45) turn up to challenge any hard-and-fast rule that each line merits its own verb.

Moseley's chapter on *signposting* recommends action verbs as a way to establish more dynamic interaction with other actors whenever one's own character "performs" what he or she wants other characters to see. I've found this premise useful for guiding students to choose bolder actions that might otherwise feel "over the top," or like indicating, or which seem to threaten to subordinate other actors during the scene. Actioning demands specificity from actors, the importance of which would be hard to underestimate.

Commendable as I find it to ply actors with means to address a range of challenges, I find it hard to support a notion that any single analytical vein can be followed faithfully and applied steadily to guarantee a superior result no matter the play at hand or the experience, or lack of it, among the collective. Empowering actors is always a good idea, and encouraging them to press a play's text closely for the sake of inspiration stands to enhance work in the making in any setting, and at least partly independent of whosoever shall direct the production. It was easier for me to see the actor-empowering properties in *Actioning* than it was in *A Director's Guide to Stanislavsky's Active Analysis,* which takes it for granted that a director needs always to be in charge.

Finally, who knows what Stanislavsky, who died in 1938, meant in any absolute or timeless sense, given our historical distance from him and his own shifts of emphasis and approach over the decades he was active? He kept changing his mind about priorities, and that's to his credit, however much confusion and dispute it has sown. That he is still used and cited so often to ground primers like Thomas's and Moselely's testifies to his ongoing importance, in the Eurocentric theater especially.

The Actor's Business Plan:
A Career Guide for the Acting Life
by Jane Drake Brody
London: Bloomsbury Methuen Drama, 2015

&

The Thriving Artist: Saving and Investing for Performers, Artists, and the Stage & Film Industries
by David Maurice Sharp
Burlington, MA; Abingdon, UK: Focal Press/ Taylor & Francis, 2015

Reviewed by Amy Guerin

How to build a sustainable career and life in the arts is the central question of both *The Actor's Business Plan: A Career Guide for the Acting Life* by Jane Drake Brody and *The Thriving Artist: Saving and Investing for Performers, Artists, and the Stage & Film Industries* by David Maurice Sharp. Brody and Sharp come at the question from two different angles—one broad, one narrow. But taken together, they provide a roadmap for early career performers to follow in order to have a life that is creatively successful, financially comfortable, and long-lasting. Their de-mystifications of the post-college life of a performer are not perfect, but they are worthwhile additions to the resources available to students and professors in upper-level professional preparation or artistic entrepreneurship classes.

Brody has worked "as an actress, casting director, acting teacher, and director" (ix). This expertise in the business side of performance, as opposed to the purely creative side, shows in her work. She writes confidently about how to network with industry professionals, what all those professionals do, and how to market oneself effectively as a performer. Sharp was trained as a dancer, with a BFA from NYU, whose temporary job with a Wall Street firm turned into a 13-year permanent, salaried position that still allowed him to pursue his dance career (Sharp 2). His knowledge of personal finances is detailed yet concise and explained with as little jargon as possible. He moves readers quickly through establishing good financial habits, and on to the myriad investment options possible, and most importantly, how one actually makes those investments happen.

While Sharp's book runs to a brisk 192 pages, including glossary and index, it is not a fast read. The information on different kinds of investment products is detailed and may be new information for some readers, requiring time to digest and understand. Sharp is as clear as he can be about the complexities of what he is writing about, but they are still complexities. Brody has the tendency to editorialize about the topics she is writing about, and not all readers may agree with her editorial statements, like this one in a discussion of personal relationships in the life of a professional actor: "Giving up on it [a romantic relationship] doesn't generally happen until we are in our late 40s" (24). These editorial statements hinder what should be a fairly straightforward explanation of her ideas for building a long-term career.

The Actor's Business Plan is laid out in the form of preparing for a play, a familiar process to the intended audience of early-career performers engaged in what Brody calls the actor's "Life Play" (1). As a part of a curriculum, as Brody explains in an opening note, the thirteen chapters include exercises that can be worked into a 14-week semester, culminating in a finished career plan as a final project. The chapters move through all the different parts of the actor's play process, from understanding given circumstances, to building a character, to the location of the performance, in a way that the information builds from one chapter to the next and methodically moves the fresh-out-of-college actor from preparation to profession. Each chapter starts with a clear introduction of the concept—a life plan, a financial plan, a networking plan—and then gives multiple examples of what those plans look like in action. Brody does very well in not just showing what a good plan looks like, but also in what a poor plan looks like, explaining why the one will work and the other won't.

Likewise, *The Thriving Artist* begins with the basics and builds to more complex financial information. The table of contents features 31 chapters, which is daunting on the face of it, but the chapters are short, some only a few pages long. A list of tables is also included for fast reference after the book has been read. After the introductory chapters, the book is organized by investment product including cash, bonds, stocks, mutual funds, and retirement funds. In between each topic are interludes that Sharp calls "Intermissions." These are quite clever, giving the reader a chance to process what he or she has just read and to directly connect performance experiences with investing. With these intermissions, Sharp synergizes information in a way that makes the performer feel more comfortable tackling the practicalities of investing.

Both Brody and Sharp organize their information in a way that takes the reader on a journey from less complex to more complex information. The reader is able to clearly see the methodical way the authors have set their paths and will be able to follow that path to the most prepared and informed version of an early-career performer possible, if not career and/or financial success (which is never guaranteed by either author or by life itself). The level of preparation that both authors lay out is rigorous and detailed, but, for those aware enough to know that a sustainable career in the theater industry demands that level of preparation, it is comforting to have everything so clearly laid out.

Brody's content is very concrete. Not one to speak in the abstract, she provides actual dollar amounts for union dues, headshot photographers, and even rent in major markets around the country. All of her budgeting content is backed up with the website or paper source where she found the information, making it possible for this book to age well over time, because a performer five years from now can access the website she cites for New York rent to check the numbers. Throughout the book are testimonials from working actors speaking about their issues in, once again, very concrete terms. One testimonial has an actor admitting "I owe Fannie Mae [a government loan agency] about $50,000" in student loans and detailing the repercussions they've faced from that debt load (Brody 61). Brody does not hide the hardships of the profession and is bold enough to say that young actors should work outside of New York and Los Angeles in smaller markets to build career experience: "Moving to L.A./NYC without union affiliations, representation, and/or experience beyond school is a really bad idea because gaining access there will take you twice as long" (Brody 82). Her clear-eyed words scrape away the romance of the starving artist dream and force young actors to think critically about the career they want to pursue, why they want to pursue it, and how, practically, they can make that happen. Her book also includes information about cover letters, websites, and reels—topics sometimes excluded from discussions about self-branding and marketing.

Like Brody, Sharp does the same kind of clear-eyed writing to break down the stereotype of the starving artist. While living in a loft in Alphabet City without electricity and refusing to pay rent makes a great musical, it doesn't make a great life. Sharp reinforces the idea again and again that, even with the sometimes meager earnings an artist makes, there is still room to create short-term financial stability and long-term financial security. As he writes in the introduction, this book came from his search to "find a way to take control of my finances and to start having them work for me instead of me always trying, and more often failing, to stay ahead of the seemingly ever-looming financial apocalypse" (Sharp xiv). Starting with the idea that being financially secure gives performers more choices on what performance opportunities they want to pursue—the artistically satisfying one versus the hold-your-nose-but-pay-your-rent one—Sharp moves through discussions of financial habits to develop, discussing risk, fundamentals, taxes (what they are and how to pay them), and the differences between banks and credit unions. He stresses the importance of what he calls a "Cash Stash" as a buffer against unexpected expenses, or as a way to afford to go to L.A. for pilot season, without racking up credit card debt. After the fundamentals are covered, he dives into the work of explaining how different investments function and how early-career performers can make those investments work for them. Similarly to Brody, he doesn't back away from recognizing the discipline that this kind of financial sustainability requires. But, his encouraging tone and personal experience make what could seem like a dream to an actor into something that is achievable by anyone, regardless of economic circumstance.

The Actor's Business Plan and *The Thriving Artist* are strong as stand-alone books that address specific needs within the artistic community. Both go beyond the performance theory and practice that students spend their college careers learning, and help calm anxiety by focusing on students after their graduation. Each author connects directly to the anxiety that performance students feel after graduation. Taken as a pair, these books, made even stronger by their pairing, are the answer to the question "I've graduated; now what?" The books are not concerned with performance talent or math prowess, but they describe those abilities as secondary to the practical entrepreneurial skills that, with practice, anyone regardless of acting talent or math capability can master.

With those positive points in mind, what the books don't do is ask questions about the ethics of the number of actors currently being trained versus the worthwhile opportunities available. While both authors assume that the decision to be a performer is immutable, as educators we must continue to wrestle with the challenges in a world that sees what we do—and what we train our students to do—as an increasingly niche product.

Ultimately, Brody and Sharp add well-written, jargon-free resources to the growing field of artistic entrepreneurship. They would be worthy additions to a class reading list and are organized in a way that makes them easy to assimilate into a curriculum. College juniors and seniors, graduate students, and teachers, would all benefit from what they have to offer to the field of performance pedagogy.

An Actor's Task: Engaging the Senses
by Baron Kelly
Indianapolis, IN: Hackett Publishing Company, 2015

Reviewed by Melissa Miller

Directors, teachers, and aspiring performers will find Baron Kelly's *An Actor's Task: Engaging the Senses* full of both innovative and familiar acting exercises. Though Kelly does not espouse one particular method, his detailed and manageable collection of warm-ups, group activities, and improvisational etudes explores a broad spectrum of actor training, synthesizing many commonalities among popular techniques. Kelly pulls from numerous foundational acting coaches including Constantin Stanislavski, Sanford Meisner, Uta Hagen, and Michael Chekhov. The result is a sort of "greatest hits" compilation, a handy guide to turn to when seeking inspiration or fleshing out lesson plans. Part performance manual, part instructor toolbox, *An Actor's Task* is a convenient reference tool for any theater practitioner.

In the preface, Kelly identifies his aim: to present a series of exercises "for students to develop a creative imagination, an ability to observe, to concentrate, and to communicate as well as to cultivate expressive tools, such as movement, speech, and voice" (xi). Delivering on this promise, Kelly presents over 100 neatly packaged and thoroughly explicated exercises for the actor. Complex concepts such as breath control, emotional memory, concentration, and imagination are explored systematically and succinctly. Exercises are grouped categorically into six distinct chapters. At the end of each exercise, Kelly poses what he refers to as "self-monitoring" questions to the performer. These guide reflections, encourage active engagement, and imply an aggregate accumulation of knowledge and skill.

Though *An Actor's Task* is primarily a collation of existing technique, Kelly's focus on self-monitoring sets his book apart from similar works such as *A Practical Handbook for the Actor*. A clear and concise focus on studio-style activities grounds Kelly's book in its classic actor training style. This author describes his theatrical exercises in such a way as to be easily understood by the theater novice. At times, this tone establishes *An Actor's Task* as a bit basic or elementary to experienced artists. However, as a potential introduction to acting textbook or high school acting handbook, *An Actor's Task* could replace or supplement staples such as Stanislavski's *An Actor Prepares* or Hagen's *Respect for Acting*. Kelly has effectively repackaged the exercises popularized by the great acting coaches, eliminating outdated references to Laurence Olivier and Laurette Taylor (of whom very few students have heard in 2017), and instead, providing a methodical how-to outline of the actor's process.

Kelly's writing is most compelling when he allows his own philosophy on acting and actor-training to emerge. *An Actor's Task* is primarily an activity reference manual, codified by theme into brief chapters. Yet Kelly deftly includes his own opinion on what he deems to be the actor's task as well. Kelly speaks from a well-deserved place of authority as both an Associate Professor of Theatre Arts and the Director of the African American Theatre Program at the University of Louisville. He claims in the book's introduction that his is a script-centered approach to acting—the actor serves the playwright. His point of view on this subject is consistent, though the majority of the foundational exercises explored are technique-oriented and do not utilize script work. In his chapter on voice, Kelly describes the actor as a unique sort of athlete, requiring practice, training, and discipline. Later in the same chapter, he simplifies the performer's job: "In short, acting is about being affected and responding" (33). These brief insights into Kelly's own acting opinions and principles help bring voice to a book that would otherwise be an anthology of technique.

Though Kelly does well to interject his own thoughts into the material presented in *An Actor's Task*, the book contains very little in terms of concrete acting theory. Though this is helpful in keeping the tone of the book accessible rather than academic, the lack of context could leave newcomers with many practical applications, but little background knowledge. While the brevity of *An Actor's Task* is appropriate, perhaps some additional narrative linking the studio activities to stage performance would enhance the applicability of Kelly's text.

An Actor's Task codifies the countless laboratory exercises rattling around in the brains of acting instructors. Having this book on the shelf will simplify the syllabus organization of any performance teacher. Kelly offers his readers a take-what-you-need approach to actor training, including suggestions for open scenes, improvisation self-starter templates, and modifications for exercises based on experience level and class size.

In some cases, these exercises would benefit from an explanatory video of examples, since multi-layered, multi-step exercises are difficult to articulate in writing (perhaps in Kelly's second edition, an accompanying DVD could be included). However, Kelly accomplishes his goal of creating an actor- and teacher-friendly workbook. *An Actor's Task* affords opportunities for actors both diving into initial exploration and those looking to enhance existing skill-sets. Kelly's book is engaging, informative, and thoroughly useful.

Acting, Imaging, and the Unconscious
by Eric Morris
Los Angeles: Ermor Enterprises, 2015

Reviewed by Ellen W. Kaplan

Acting, Imaging, and the Unconscious is the fifth book in a series by well-known acting teacher Eric Morris, who has been active in the profession for over fifty years. Morris is a former head of the Directors Unit of the Actors Studio in Los Angeles and is acknowledged as a foremost interpreter of Lee Strasberg's method. This book builds on the material in Morris' previous volumes, and a working knowledge of his "System" is a prerequisite for fully digesting what he offers here.

Morris' work is based on Stanislavski's seminal theories, particularly as developed by Lee Strasberg, first in the Group Theatre, then later in the Actors Studio. Morris's somewhat controversial system addresses what he feels needs development and finer articulation in Strasberg's method. In Morris' earlier books, particularly *No Acting Please*, *Being and Doing*, and *Irreverent Acting*, he offers a methodical, hands-on approach that addresses "instrument" and "craft." Instrument refers to the actor's body, mind, emotional life, memories, and imagination; precisely detailed exercises are geared to relieving tension, overcoming psychic blocks, and building confidence and self-esteem. Craft refers to technique applied to dramatic text, with a focus on what he calls "choices" (points of focus) and the "obligations" (given circumstances) of the play.

Morris emphasizes truthful, sensory-rich, organic acting. In seeking to create authentic experience on the stage, he offers a systematic approach to acting through sense memory and affective memory. The goal is to release actors so they are unhampered by the emotional inhibitions and self-consciousness that lead to stifled impulses and clichéd acting. Morris wants actors to become what he calls "professional experiencers" (9), who live every moment truthfully on the stage, achieving what he jocularly calls "the eleventh level of consciousness" (151).

Acting, Imaging, and the Unconscious focuses on two important tools: *imaging* (an alternate term for *creative visualization*, a technique long used by actors, athletes and others) and *sense memory*. Morris puts forward a powerful thesis, that visualization is most helpful and best accomplished by immersive, sensory engagement with personal memories, dreams, and fantasies. He aims to present techniques that integrate visualization and sense memory. Morris lays out his goals in the introduction, saying he explores "imaging in all the ways it relates to acting: as preparation, as a choice approach, and as a way to get down deeper into oneself and to use the unconscious to inspire and 'dimensionalize' one's work" (6). Sensory engagement is key, allowing the actor to move out of verbalizing experience into fulfilling it. This is presented as a tool for personal growth and achievement, as well as a means for freeing the actor. Ultimately, Morris asserts that these processes offer access to the unconscious, and he devotes a significant portion of this book to developing that pathway.

The book is replete with exercises that aim to stimulate the creative process by harnessing the power of sense and affective memory, and imagination. Morris offers a step-by-step description of practices that utilize specific techniques of imaging "for pleasure or fantasy, as a motivational tool, or as a process for creating emotional life on the stage" (21). Combining sense memory with imaging helps the actor work truthfully, without involving the intellect. The central point Morris makes is that imaging, "when combined with the sensorial approach . . . becomes a humongous force in the creative process" (25). This is an area of actor training not always addressed in mainstream techniques.

There is, however, only nominal attention given to addressing what Morris calls the "obligations" (10) of the script. Morris trains the actor's imagination and emotional availability, but his system, as articulated in this book, seems to skirt the text, touching only lightly on character, story, and dramatic action. The emphasis is almost exclusively on accessing the actor's emotions. But emotion on stage is a byproduct of playing action, in service to objectives, and to moment-to-moment, reciprocal relationships. Working so intently on what the actor feels, as opposed to what she or he does, can take the actor out of the immediate moment and make her unresponsive to the given circumstances of the play. This undermines the playfulness and responsiveness that characterize the best work on stage.

Morris asks the actor to draw on personal relationships and parallel circumstances from life to create the relationships in a play; character actions and subtext are created by the actor's prior experience or memory, which function as substitutions or endowments. Inherent in his system is that the work becomes more a statement of self than story; of playing oneself over and over again, rather than rising to the demands of genre, style, poetry, and drama that are larger than life. There is no mention of intentions and actions, of structure, or of the world of the play as created by the writer. Given circumstances, what Morris calls the "obligations of the text" (10), are alluded to, but rarely analyzed or investigated. There are sections, such as explorations of Amanda Wingfield and Willy Loman, where the techniques are applied to character, but these are almost incidental within the book.

Morris encourages actors to daydream, to fantasize, and imagine freely, while bringing the full sensory apparatus into play. These are great ideas, and the methods help move the actor from a clinical, cognitive analysis into a full sensory experience. But there is an over-emphasis on the internal experience of the actor. When the actor draws on prior memories rather than the imaginary circumstances of the play, stage life is diminished.

To experience what the character is experiencing is a difficult concept to parse: no one knows exactly what a character is experiencing, and what matters is that the actor is engaged and personally invested in enacting the character, manifested through actions, decisions, deliberations, and responses. The tangible evidence of the character is in what she or he says and does, not what she or he feels. If a character is angry, the actor might try to generate that feeling by creating an inner monologue based on a memory of a past experience. But affective memory, like substitution, can take the actor out of the moment on stage.

The book is organized into eight chapters, beginning in chapter 1 with a brief discussion of Morris' system. The rest of the book explores imaging in a wide range of contexts. Chapter 2 is devoted to the "what, how and why" of imaging. Chapter 3 offers detailed descriptions and samples of seven distinct imaging techniques (Involuntary, Symbolic, Fragmented, Free-Association, Story, Verbalized, and Guided Imaging), followed by a sub-section titled "Fantasy Imaging" which discusses "Using Fantasy to Elevate the Imagination" (76-81). Among the techniques offered in this chapter are some which involve working with acting partners. This is of special interest for rehearsals and classroom scene work.

In chapter 5, the reader is introduced to specific ways that imaging can be applied to acting. Morris reviews his concepts of choice and obligation. He uses a specialized vocabulary to describe techniques drawn from his Method, which can add unnecessary confusion for those not fully versed in his system. For example, "Imaging" may be a "Choice Approach with Different Obligations" (126), including "Time and Place," "Relationship," "Emotional," and "Character Obligations," among others (127, 132, 141, 153). The vocabulary gets complicated—there are 26 "choice approaches," for example (63, 126)—and can become an obstacle to smooth incorporation of his techniques into the actor's routine.

Chapter 6, "Imaging and Sub-Personalities," offers a brief look at types (labeled as Jungian archetypes) which inhabit us: the Critic, the Achiever, the Victim, and others. This is a useful tool for character analysis, and brought into the actor's personal work can be revelatory. From here on, Morris discusses ways of accessing the unconscious and harnessing the impulses that arise from sub- or unconscious reservoirs of feeling, memory, and stimuli. In chapters 7 and 8, respectively "Imaging and the Unconscious" and "Programming the Unconscious," Morris discusses how "communicating with the unconscious" (247) can offer a wealth of riches for the actor, and he presents his methodology for doing so. The actor is encouraged to recall and investigate dreams, to create a dream journal, and to identify and talk with characters in the dreams. This rich territory is explored by few acting teachers (Janet Sonenberg's Dreamwork for Actors is a notable exception), and is of great value to the expressive artist.

I came away from *Acting, Imaging, and the Unconscious* somewhat skeptical. I find Morris's earlier books indispensable for a basic training routine, as he breaks down and expands upon basic Method acting principles and offers clear descriptions of exercises to develop sense memory, characterization, improvisation, and other tools for the actor. In *Acting, Imaging, and the Unconscious* he thoroughly investigates imaging, and helps the actor "get out of his/her head," But there is no mention of listening, playing tasks, pursuing objectives, or discovering the life of the character. Also, Morris's terminology can be an obstacle for the reader who isn't fully conversant with his system; he renames commonly understood terms such as sense memory, affective memory, substitution, and endowment, among others. It takes some time to translate Morris's ideas into more familiar language, even though the ideas are parallel or replicate the normative terminology.

This volume contributes some new ideas and offers precise guidance for utilizing this aspect of Morris's system. Compared to his earlier work, however, this book is a difficult read, a sclerotic and attenuated treatment of much of the same material covered previously. The tone can be overly simplistic, as he cheerleads his readers to "expand their consciousness." In addition, the book needs significant editing. Grammatical errors, misuse of words, ungainly sentences, and long, unnecessarily complicated examples make reading the book something of a chore. An editor would also chop up the thicket of exclamation points, which clutter the book throughout. While the precise descriptions of exercises are useful, the personal examples are over-written and tend to swamp the book.

As Morris asserts, "Imaging is probably the most commonly used technique in acting" (37). This is certainly true, and the idea that imaging should be done with full engagement of the senses is superb. But the thesis doesn't need the systematic elaborations offered here; it is an excellent insight, but a simpler, more concise explication would serve better. When Morris says, for example, that "the seven techniques of imaging are part of the 26th choice approach" (63), he is using jargon that is daunting and off-putting for readers not thoroughly familiar with his entire system.

Sensory images can be powerful triggers or springboards into imaginative engagement with the circumstances of the play, and as such are tremendously powerful. This brings to mind an old anecdote about Group Theatre actor Morris Carnovsky. In the play *Success Story*, Carnovsky played Rufus, a character considering suicide. Each night, the audience would gasp when Carnovsky put a gun to his head. When asked what went through his mind, the actor said he thought of the moment when he was about to step into a cold shower. The shock of the icy water brought alive the moment when he was about to pull the trigger at his head. This brilliant use of sense memory perhaps is the best example of what Morris's system can offer the actor.

Acting, Archetype, and Neuroscience: Superscenes for Rehearsal and Performance
by Jane Drake Brody
London: Routledge, 2017

Reviewed by Jeffrey Toth and Charles Grimes

What if there were a way for actors to perform on stage in such a fashion as to directly manipulate the brain activity of their audience, and by doing so, pull them deeper into the experience and meaning of a theatrical production? And what if there were a method by which acting coaches could "move actors into the less accessible regions of themselves and release hotter, more dangerous, and less literal means of approaching a role?" (Brody book jacket). Well, in the short, quirky, and somewhat uneven *Acting, Archetype, and Neuroscience: Superscenes for Rehearsal and Performance*, Jane Drake Brody claims we can do just that. It is simply a matter of honing actors' psychological impulses and physical movements so that they tap into the brain's recently discovered mirror neuron system; refining actors' use of language to engage the metaphorical, action-based, embodied meanings that underlie all communication; and getting them in touch with the heroes, myths, and archetypes that Brody believes underlie all dramatic writing. Clearly something new is afoot in theatrical training.

Jane Brody, a former Associate Professor of Performance at The Theater School of DePaul University who retired in 2015, has written an interesting, albeit challenging and sometimes frustrating book that touches on the topics above as well as "superscenes," her own training method for getting actors to "move past personality and into biology and impulse as motivating forces" (89). Part history, part speculative science essay, part theatrical-training exercise guide, *Acting, Archetype, and Neuroscience* attempts to weave together both a method and a science-based rationale for creating more powerful forms of theater. And, in general, she succeeds, at least in getting one to see the potential of an ongoing collaboration between neuroscience and the performing arts, while offering potent and provocative tools for script analysis, actor training, and scene work.

The book is divided into three sections. Along with the introductory comments, part 1, "Origins," provides Brody's rationale for writing the book, her concerns with current actor training, and her longstanding focus on the role of myth, archetypes, and the hero's journey as motivating structures in literature. This first section also offers Brody's perspective on current research in neuroscience, including the discovery of mirror neurons, brain cells that participate in the execution of a motor action as well the perception of someone else performing that action. Although well-established in constrained laboratory contexts, mirror neurons have also been the source of considerable speculation, that they are the basis of empathy, for example, or the understanding of another's intentions. This has earned them a somewhat dubious reputation among neuroscientists. Brody is aware of this controversy and thus advances a relatively limited interpretation of mirror neurons, primarily suggesting that "action, reaction, and intention" are at the heart of good theater (29). Her desire to relate ideas from disparate disciplines, along with the resonance of the connections she makes between theater and neuroscience, allows the reader to feel that an interesting and provocative book is on offer.

Part 2, "The Exercises and the Work," is a series of step-by-step procedures for implementing Brody's approach to actor training. These exercises begin with meditation (detailed instructions are included), and then move on to more action-oriented exercises designed to get actors to explore their visceral responses to events. These include the essential psychophysical actions of "push, pull, hold, and release" as designed by Lecoq and interpreted by Paul Kassel, along with exercises that encourage actors to interact with their partners in ways that enhance conflict and responsiveness. For example, borrowing from the Viewpoints technique (which she traces to the choreographer Mary Overlie), Brody encourages trainers to physicalize elemental actions "as a means of training actors in spontaneity, physical commitment, ensemble building, sensory awareness, self-discovery, and embodied creativity" (56).

Readers may sense that a lifetime of engagement with theater has been distilled in this book, as the author offers a range of practical advice as well as provocative thoughts about how the human psyche is structured. Part 2 also includes Brody's psycho dynamically-informed script analysis along with physical exercises that follow from that method. Relying heavily on Joseph Campbell's work *The Power of Myth*, she advocates reading all plays and characters as examples of the hero's journey—a cycle in which a hero separates from his normal environment, takes on an extraordinary task, is met by helpers and enemies, and finally returns, transformed, to an altered world. Subsequent chapters in this section expand upon and contextualize the hero's journey, including detailed examples of Muhammad Ali's life story and the play *Hamlet*. Brody wisely encourages debate and discussion of these journeys rather than imposing a singular interpretation. She does note, though without as much elaboration as some might desire, that archetypal criticism tends to privilege male figures and masculinist meanings (75). Brody adds to her script analysis approach by suggesting that all plays embody a "primary conflict" between chaos and order (38), and maintains that any archetypal conflict between characters endures past the end of a play (74).

Script analysis centered on the hero's journey serves as a prerequisite to superscenes, "exercises in which actors physically explore the archetypal conflicts in the essential relationships of the text in a fully physical way" (89). These superscenes, discussed at the end of part 2, are an exciting tool for converting an actor's reservoir of spirit, impulse, and primal/archetypal feeling into production or scene work. In superscenes, actors start by correlating the character they are playing with an archetype or mythical figure. She uses the example of Diana the huntress (86). Actors create physical gestures and movements inspired by aspects of this figure, and then use these postures to manifest psychological connections with their scene partners, physicalizing their conflict through kinesthetic responses, finally adding in phrases from the script at hand (86-95). Here, Brody offers a way for actors to engage with ideas of conflict and energy in a primal, action-oriented, pre-linguistic form that, with the assistance of mirror neurons, promises to release deeper, more intense performances.

From an instructional perspective, the theater professor reviewing this book sees a red flag when Brody asserts that "full body contact is necessary" and that scene partners are to "move impulsively from protective ideas to murderous impulses to sexual feelings" (90, 91). Actor safety may be an issue when such impulsivity is encouraged.

Part 3, "Neuroscience and Images," returns to many of the themes laid out in part 1, including the limbic system, meditation, and mirror neurons. It is in this section that Brody, quoting liberally from a wide range of practicing neuroscientists and philosophers (including Antonio Damasio, Giacomo Rizolatti, and Daniel Dennett), makes her strongest case for increased interaction between neuroscience and theater. Mirror neurons, brain cells which mediate both the performance and observational understanding of an action, are at the heart of Brody's argument and receive their most systematic discussion in this section. The vision Brody advances is compelling: if an actor's physical actions can activate analogous, intention-bearing brain circuits in observers, then experiencing a play can become a real, visceral, embodied experience, taking audience members deep into the heart of the action. Good acting, derived from and connected to unconscious impulses (enhanced via superscenes), will activate mirror neurons in the brains of audience members, providing them with more emotional, sub-rational connections with an actor's performance. Patterns of behavior, she further asserts, can be read in terms of fundamental or archetypal forms of human experience. Part 3 thus reverts to themes of archetype, myth, and plot, and Brody includes a chapter on the mythical structure of Suzan-Lori Parks's *In the Blood*, and offers models of archetypal plot patterns from Georges Polti, Denis Johnson, and Christopher Booker.

While physical action is clearly at the core of Brody's approach, she also discusses text and textual meaning. Her perspective is informed by research in the fields of embodied cognition and embodied semantics which claim that, not only is most/all language metaphorical, but that metaphors are understood through the specific, material ways in which our bodies, brains, and social selves are embedded and situated in the world. George Lakoff and Mark Johnson's *Metaphors We Live By* is discussed here. In terms of its application to theater, and similar to the notion of mirror neurons, Brody makes the important point that an actor's understanding and delivery of lines, as well as the imagery those lines evoke, will have decisive neuropsychological implications for how a performance is experienced by the audience (e.g., as hot and visceral versus cold and intellectual).

In contrast to those interesting ideas, much of the neuroscience in this book is either incorrect (such as the claim that the modern study of memory was driven by Freudian and Jungian psychology [116-17]) or overly romanticized. Thus when Brody claims that mirror neurons are part of the process by which archetypes guide us through infancy (124), or asserts that myths and archetypes are "representations of both the reptilian and the primal brain" (32), she moves well beyond available evidence and makes statements few neuroscientists would abide. She also has a habit of including long scientific quotations with little contextualization, leaving many of the central ideas under-explained to non-specialists. And she can seem in a rush to assert the validity of novel neuroscientific concepts. For example, the claim that mirror neurons "have changed the entire face of the cognitive science community" (111) is at odds with both the makeup of that discipline (much of which addresses questions for which motor neurons are irrelevant) and the critical reception that mirror neurons have met in some quarters (see, e.g., Gregory Hickok's *The Myth of Mirror Neurons*). Conversely, from a theatre artist's perspective, Brody's tone seems to oversell her idea that action is interactive, having to do with what one character wants from another. This notion is closer to a truism than an innovation in acting theory, and many readers will already agree with it, without seeing a need to ground this understanding in archetypal or cognitive psychology.

Nevertheless, there are enough novel and provocative ideas here to sustain the interested student of neurotheater, as well as the acting coach or director seeking new ways to conceive of dramatic conflict and communication. For example, consideration of the James-Lange theory of emotion—the idea that emotional stimuli trigger behavioral and autonomic activity prior to subjective feeling—leads to clear suggestions for theatrical training, such as getting actors to grasp that when an emotional event occurs, their bodies and actions should lead while their cognitive understanding and verbal statements follow.

Beyond the sense that Brody does not support all her claims, readers may experience some structural confusion while perusing the book. She has a habit of mentioning an idea and then returning to it pages later without acknowledging or explicitly building on that first mention. The discussion of superscenes does not explicitly appear until chapter 7 and even there it takes up only half the chapter. Her chapter on *In the Blood* contains the line "If I were reading this book, I might be tempted to skip this chapter" (138), which leads one to wonder why she did not then solve that organizational issue. The section on archetypal plot patterns, near the end of the book, is mostly quotation with very little explanation, which makes these ideas appear something of an afterthought. And, at the risk of sounding like a quibbler, more than a few names are misspelled or spelled inconsistently.

Despite its flaws, *Acting, Archetype, and Neuroscience* is both novel and interesting in its attempt to meld archetypal psychology, contemporary neuroscience, and theories of embodied language into a complex and vital presence in the landscape of actor training. Although the book's reach often exceeds its grasp, it nevertheless reaches out in several valuable directions. As such, its content should draw necessary attention to other authors exploring the intersection of neuroscience, embodied cognition, and theater (see, e.g., the edited volume, *Theater and Cognitive Neuroscience*, and the work of Amy Cook, Joseph Roach, and Rhonda Blair) while also offering valuable ways to read scripts, launch a production, or gain new insights into the scenes the reader teaches and rehearses. Brody's book thus opens a route to an important and lofty goal: developing scientifically-supported methods for creating rich, spontaneous, visceral performances that electrify audiences and exemplify the highest potential of theater.

Black Acting Methods: Critical Approaches
by Sharrell D. Luckett and Tia M. Shaffer
London: Routledge, 2016

Reviewed by Amber Jaunai

Black Acting Methods: Critical Approaches is composed of articles written by several contributors and is spearheaded by Sharrel D. Luckett and Tia M. Shaffer. Dr. Luckett is an award-winning director and assistant professor of theater and performance studies focused in performance theory, black studies, and women studies at Muhlenberg College, in Allentown, Pennsylvania. Her counterpart, Tia M. Shaffer, is a fine arts chair and theater director at South Atlanta High School as well as a director for youth and children's ministries at Zion Hill Baptist Church. Both authors grew up in Atlanta, Georgia, the "Black Mecca," and participated in several theater and social activist programs throughout their careers. In the opening affirmations, Shaffer and Luckett declare that this anthology is for all actors and educators, of all backgrounds, as it emphasizes the importance of cultivating racially and culturally diverse spaces when training young artists, especially black artists. This proclamation goes hand in hand with the central theme of black culture, appropriately emphasized by each contributor: the power of unity, community, and inclusion.

Shaffer and Luckett gather a team of scholars to expand on their relationship to black performance art, specifically in America, since African-American work tends to be a source of healing for the black community. Black artists are forced to create their own material and safe spaces to present their work, often in response to the detrimental and limiting roles they are reduced to in the mainstream society. Subsequently, almost all of the writers address how they approached dismantling the constraining stereotypes most artists of color find themselves imprisoned to today. Afrocentricity, Africanizing, Afrofuturism, and the spirit of collectivism are among some of the concepts shared and explored, which empower young artists to connect to their sense of self and creative integrity. Black art endows us with the power to re-connect to our African heritage, which has been eradicated during centuries of slavery, as well as to re-conceptualize the way our image is projected in mainstream culture, intrinsically empowering the next generation.

Artists, educational heads, scholars, and directors are among the contributors who provide insight to black acting pedagogy as well as how they put these skills to practice. This anthology has a spiritually-secular feeling as each article is referred to as an offering, which "align(s) with black African customs and culture, as the notion of giving is innately ingrained in the 'fiber of our being.'" Admittedly, it is sometimes hard to follow along when there are multiple writers for an article, for example, in the opening affirmation, the voice often haphazardly changes in respect to the speaker.

In the vein of social activist approaches, the first offering, written by Luckett and Shaffer, explains the Hendricks Method created by Freddie Hendricks: the methodical foundation of the highly awarded and widely recognized Youth Ensemble of Atlanta (co-created by Hendricks and his close friends). The professional acting company, comprised of actors ages eight to twenty-four, focuses on devising socially and politically relevant musicals. The Hendricks Method successfully develops intelligent artists by providing members with the space to embody and understand the topics they explore, requiring them to bring in research, adopting an "on your feet" and repetitive rehearsal process, and making them take responsibility for honoring their cultural and self identity. Possibly the most important component of the Hendricks Method, in my opinion, is the hyper ego as it nurtures a sense of confidence that combats the need of validation that plagues actors of color, from a world and industry that constantly tells us that we can't.

The next social activist offering, "Soul Work," by Cristal Chanelle Truscott, describes the philosophy of shifting the focus of theater-making from the individual to the collective. "Soul Work" inspires endless exploration and a continuous call and response between the individual, community, and society as a whole. Truscott reclaims her "soul" after years of colorblind training that attempted to erase her cultural identity except when requisitioned for "Black" roles. With "Soul Work," Truscott encourages artists to contribute their cultural, religious, and intellectual specificity to enrich the ensemble, creating a cross-cultural dialogue and awareness—which also makes it applicable to a variation of artistic mediums such as playwriting, composing, and directing.

The third offering, "Nudging the Memory" by Rhodessa Jones, spotlights The Medea Project, which has created a strong community and outlet for incarcerated women, specifically African-American women, who are "the largest growing population in the penal system," and Latin American women who run a "close second." Jones provides a safe environment for these women to play and claim both the negative and positive aspects of their lives in the hope of reducing the number of second offenders. With over twelve productions and a transatlantic reach and impact on the theater scene, The Medea Project proves to be a success in raising women's sense of self-worth as well as raising community awareness to the power theater has on breaking the cycle of incarceration. Similarly, Lisa Biggs explains how improvisation taught from the Black feminist perspective highlights injustices by giving a voice to the voiceless, who in turn create a public discourse in the hopes of making a social change as outlined in her offering: "Art Saves Lives."

The section of interventional methods was the most personally inspiring as it perfectly articulated the shortcomings that I, as well as some of my peers, experienced while being trained in a program with a strong foundation in Eurocentric techniques. I connected to the writers who expressed a lack of preparedness and inspiration when entering the industry as their formal training failed to acknowledge or nurture their racial and cultural identity. For example, Justin Emeka's offering, "Seeing Shakespeare through Brown Eyes," debunks the effectiveness of colorblind casting while advocating the power of examining classical (white) texts through different cultural lenses. Although colorblindness was originally effective in being inclusive as it offered opportunities for actors of color to be cast in traditionally white roles, it is equated to stripping their cultural specificity in order to fit in a "universal" world defined by whiteness. It is impossible not to see race, yet many people fail to acknowledge the long history of racial injustice and problematically associate disregard for progressiveness. I interpreted Emeka's argument as an opportunity to view characters as colorblind while acknowledging an actor's racial and cultural individualism to enrich the character and its newfound dynamic when telling a story.

In the same vein, Tawnya Pettiford-Wates reflects on the strong yet hegemonic training she received at Carnegie Mellon which created a disconnect for her when encountering material interwoven within her cultural continuum. Pettiford-Wates reiterates the importance of incorporating an actor's identity, especially in training, to help actors to become self-actualized authentic performers, directors, writers, etc. To do so, she offers a method of training, "Ritual Poetic Drama," specifically within the African Continuum to adequately train actors to embrace their entire spiritual and cultural spectrum while making them aware of their artistic integrity and societal impact. Clinnesha D. Sibley goes a step further in her offering, "Remembering, Rewriting, and Re-imaging," by providing tips for directors who direct Afrocentric pieces as well as tips on how to interact with and serve actors of color during the rehearsal process.

In the last segment of offerings, "Methods of Cultural Plurality," social activism and intervention fuse. Through cultural plurality, artists are capacitated with the ability to relate to different cultural perspectives. For example, Daniel Banks encouraged three of his NYU students' interest in hip hop theater by incorporating it into their training program essentially granting the students agency and degree credit. Banks' efforts helped create the Hip Hop Initiative that merged two innovative programs: devised theater and hip hop theater. Banks required the students to research the social justice beginnings of hip hop and its healing capabilities of transgenerational suffering in order to have a well-rounded understanding of the work they were creating. He encourages educational and communal institutions to trust the youth by supplying them with the opportunities and skills to discuss and create work that addresses personal topics in new inventive mediums.

Kashi Johnson and Daphnie Sicre further emphasize the need for inclusive spaces that celebrate and adapt to the communal and individual identity. Johnson and Sicre infuse hip hop theatre with theater of the oppressed by Augusto Boal to go beyond modern day "hashtag activism" and give students agency to express their frustrations and confront injustices both on stage and in the growing digital media. They also adopt educational concepts from Paulo Freire, the Brazilian educator who believes that the teacher and student can learn from each other appropriately informing how the curriculum is taught. In this idea, both professors utilize Facebook and other social media platforms in teaching students (due to the platforms' accessibility and high exposure) as well as publicizing the work the students create.

Branching out of the American theater landscape, Aku Kadogo created the Kadogo Mojo Method, which combines her anthropological work and cultural encounters while traveling with theater, music, and poetry. She specifically discusses her work with the indigenous people of Australia and her efforts to help them create art that defined and helped release emotions about their unjust circumstances. Her practice emphasizes the ritualistic effects of theater as it invigorates and heals by exchanging energy between the audience and performers that can be interpreted in any way necessary to the individual.

The anthology concludes with reflections and words of wisdom from distinguished practitioners. Many of the quotes were applicable to my journey as an actor especially after being awoken by this book. For example, director Shirley Jones captures how I felt before reading this book: "most actors become so busy pursuing a dream that they lose their sense of self. I have seen many Black actors lose their identity while trying to become a carbon copy of what someone else wants them to be." And director, playwright, and dramaturg,

Talvin Wilks, reminds me that I am a "part of an incredible history of groundbreaking artists who fought against staggering odds to have a place in an American tradition that often stereotypes, caricatures, mocks, ridicules, segregates and demeans the Black image on stage. Understand your history. Seek it out. Find your forefathers and foremothers and celebrate them."

Despite many of the accomplishments of these scholars and the impacts they have had in the theater community, little attention has been drawn to their contributions. *Black Acting Methods: Critical Approaches* is incredibly useful as it creates a framework for Black acting pedagogy and practical uses that is both advantageous for Black actors pursuing a career in the theater arts, as well as educational institutions that are looking to create diverse classrooms that represent our society today. I am grateful for my training and all I've learned, but I wish I had a book like this when I first entered school to guide me in a program in which I sometimes felt lost. I encourage all of my acting, directing, and writing colleagues to read this book as it has fed my soul with inspiration and a newfound understanding of my power as a young actor of color. I couldn't possibly summarize all of the discoveries, historical context, and teachings of each of the offerings, so please do yourself a favor and pick up a copy of *Black Acting Methods: Critical Approaches* and further your cultural awakening.

Notes on Contributors

Jenn Ariadne Calvano, PhD, explores movement-based actor training pedagogy as Assistant Professor of Acting and Movement at the University of Louisville Theatre Arts Department. She enjoys training the artist-scholars in the MFA program there. She earned her PhD in theater from the University of Colorado, Boulder. Her scholarly work focuses on movement-based actor training pedagogy and on examining commonalities among various approaches. Her first article will be published in the January edition of the *Journal of Dance Education*. "What Are You Looking at?—The Complication of the Male Gaze in Fin de Siècle Cancan and Fosse's *Sweet Charity*" aims to re-contextualize sexualized performance.

Suzanne Delle is an assistant professor and the theater division coordinator at York College of Pennsylvania. She has a MFA in directing from the Catholic University of America and has trained with SITI Company, Elevator Repair Service, and other companies that create their own work. In addition to her teaching and directing duties at YCP, Delle is the co-coordinator of the Fringe Festival at the KCACTF Region 2 Festival and recently presented at the Arts in Society conference in Paris.

Isaac Littlejohn Eddy lives in Vermont and teaches theater at Johnson State College. He has performed with *Blue Man Group* as a Blue Man for twelve years in New York, Las Vegas, Chicago, and was a member of the original cast in London. He also is a cartoonist and animator and has been published in *The New Yorker*, *The New York Times*, and *Time Magazine*. Isaac received an MFA degree at CUNY, Brooklyn College in performance and interactive media art. You can find his work at: IsaacLittlejohnEddy.com.

Matt Fotis is Chair of the Theatre Department and Director of Undergraduate Research at Albright College. He is the author of *Long Form Improvisation and American Comedy: The Harold*, and the co-author of *The Comedy Improv Handbook: A Comprehensive Guide to University Improvisational Comedy in Theatre and Performance*.

His work has appeared in *Theatre Journal*, *Theatre Topics*, *The Journal of American Drama and Theatre*, *The Encyclopedia of Humor Studies*, and MLB.com among others.

Charles Grimes teaches in the Department of Theatre at the University of North Carolina, Wilmington, where he is the department's dramaturg, and associate editor and book review editor of *Methods*. He is also the author of *Harold Pinter's Politics: A Silence Beyond Echo* and of articles on Peter Barnes and Bernard Shaw. He has taught at Deep Springs College, the Telluride Association, New York University, Pace University, and other schools. He has directed over thirty productions.

Amy Guerin is on the faculty at the University of Alabama in Huntsville. She previously taught at Texas A&M. In 2009, Amy's production of *A Midsummer Night's Dream*, showcasing flying fairy robots alongside human actors, was featured in *Wired* magazine, and on NPR's *Science Friday*. She has also directed *Lend Me a Tenor*, *Les Liaisons Dangereuses*, *The Conduct of Life*, *Bus Stop*, *Measure for Measure*, *An Ideal Husband*, *Tartuffe*, *Machinal*, *Wittenberg*, and *I and You*. She blogs about theater at discoballtartuffe.wordpress.com. Amy received her BFA from the University of Oklahoma, and her MFA from the University of Houston.

Amber Jaunai is a Brooklyn-based actor and collaborator. She recently graduated with a BFA in Acting from Pace University and was the recipient of the academic excellence award for her major. You can check out her upcoming and past work at amberjaunai.com.

Ellen W. Kaplan is professor of acting and directing at Smith College, and was a Fulbright Scholar in Costa Rica, Romania, and Hong Kong. Much of her work has been an exploration of creativity and trauma, and engaging with underserved communities and societies in conflict. She performs and directs internationally and has been guest professor at Tel Aviv University, Hong Kong University, The Chinese University of Hong Kong, University of Costa Rica, and The

National University of Theatre and Cinematography in Bucharest, Romania. Kaplan's plays have been presented in New York, California, Ohio, North Carolina, Connecticut, and most recently in Florida.

Adrienne Kapstein is a collaborative theater maker specializing in the creation of highly visual, interdisciplinary, physical performance. Her work has been presented in the United States, Canada, Ireland, Scotland, and Romania. Highlights include: *Light, A Dark Comedy* (The Duke on 42nd Street, New Victory LabWorks), *Washeteria* (Soho Rep), *Love is Love* (Sibiu International Theatre Festival), *Every Day Above Ground* (PS 122), and *Fathom* (Project Arts Center, Dublin). Adrienne was the Associate Director of Movement and Horse Choreography on *War Horse* (Broadway and national tours). She is currently an associate artist with Trusty Sidekick Theater Company and will be creating a new show with them to premiere in 2019. Adrienne is an associate professor at Pace School of Performing Arts teaching ensemble creation and physical theater. Her education includes studies at University of Edinburgh, Ecole Jacques Lecoq, and Brooklyn College, where she earned her MFA in Directing.

Melissa Miller is a graduate student in theater performance and pedagogy at Texas Tech University. She holds a bachelor's degree in theater performance from Wichita State University. Melissa began her master's degree in order to explore the relationship between academics and art. She currently teaches Introduction to Acting for Non-majors at TTU and is performing for the second year in ATHE's New Play Development Workshop. Melissa engages arts in her community alongside members of the Tech Feminist Majority Leadership Alliance and through student-led performances with the Burkhart Center for Autism Education and Research. Melissa has previously published articles in *The Texas Tech Daily Toreador* and *Texas Theatre Journal*.

Jessie L. Mills is a BKT Assistant Professor of Theater at Wabash College and a professional director. She specializes in ensemble theater, global comedy, new and devised works, and canonical adaptations.

Tracey Moore is currently associate professor at The Hartt School Theatre, University of Hartford. She is the author of *Acting the Song* and *Student Companion to Acting the Song* (Allworth and Skyhorse Press). Her articles and essays have appeared in *The New York Times*, *The Chronicle of Higher Education*, the journal *Studies in Musical Theatre*, *Teaching Theatre Journal*, and *Dramatics* magazine. Tracey is editor-in-chief of *Music Theater Educators' Alliance* journal. Performance credits include two Broadway national tours (*Ragtime*, *Camelot*), Off-Broadway productions (*I Will Come Back*, *Regina*, *Señor Discretion*), and leading roles in regional theaters across the country. She holds a BM in Voice from Indiana University, an MA in Dramatic Literature from Southern Illinois University, and an MFA in Acting from Brooklyn College.

Dennis Schebetta is assistant professor and head of the MFA Performance Pedagogy Program at the University of Pittsburgh. Professionally he has worked as an actor, playwright, dramaturg, and director in both film and theater. His credits include work in regional theater and Off-Off Broadway at the Ensemble Studio Theatre, at the Vital Theatre Company, Pittsburgh Playhouse, Bricolage Production Company, City Theatre Company, 13th Street Repertory Company, 12 Peers Theater and the HERE Arts Center. He trained as an actor in the two-year Meisner program with William Esper at his studio in New York and most recently studied with master Shakespeare teacher John Basil. Dennis has taught Shakespeare as a teaching artist for the Pittsburgh Public Theatre and has taught at Carnegie Mellon University, Bellevue College, and Virginia Commonwealth University where he earned his MFA in Theatre Pedagogy.

Bara Swain serves as the creative consultant at Urban Stages. Her plays have been performed across the country in more than 100 venues in 19 states. Publishers include Smith and Kraus, ArtAge Publications, and Applause Theatre & Cinema Books. *Critical Care*, produced on stage and in film, is reprinted in the college textbook *Serious Daring: Creative Writing in Four Genres* by Lisa Roney (Oxford UP) and serves as key reading for the craft of playwriting. Honors include Heideman Award finalist, *Aboard the Guy V. Molinari*; City Theatre National Award finalist for short playwriting for *The Hotel Lobbyist*; and, by special invitation from Burt Reynolds, *An Evening With Bara Swain*, directed by The Bandit (www.BaraSwain.org).

Jeffrey Toth is a cognitive neuroscientist who studies memory, attention, and executive functions. He received his PhD at the University of North Carolina Greensboro, did postdoctoral work at McMaster University and the Rotman Research Institute, was an assistant professor at Georgia Tech, a research associate at Washington University in St. Louis, and is currently an associate professor in psychology at the University of North Carolina, Wilmington. Jeff has published over 30 articles on the topics of memory, attention, aging, and the brain. He is currently exploring the brain's default mode network using functional near-infrared spectroscopy.

Leigh Woods has taught at the University of Michigan since 1987 and has served as head of theater studies during that time. He's written extensively about performance and the history of acting in *Garrick Claims the Stage*, *On Playing Shakespeare*, *Public Selves/Political Stages* (with Ágústa Gunnarsdóttir), and *Transatlantic Stage Stars in Vaudeville and Variety*. He co-edited *Playing to the Camera*, and his articles have appeared in *Theatre Survey*, *Theatre Journal*, *Scandinavian Review*, *Shakespeare Quarterly*, *Shakespeare Yearbook*, *Essays in Theatre*, *Theatre Research International*, *New Theatre Quarterly*, *The Arthur Miller Journal*, and *Contemporary Theatre Review*. A member of Actors' Equity Association, he's performed over 100 roles onstage, including American premieres of plays by George W. D. Trow, Heiner Müller, and Wendy Wasserstein. Most recently, Leigh played Leonato in *Much Ado About Nothing*.

Call for Essays, Book Reviews, and Editors

Methods is a new, peer-reviewed journal on actor training being published annually by Pace University Press. The journal aims to promote and disseminate research on all matters related to the training of actors: new exercises, innovative techniques and philosophies, discussion of principal texts and methodologies; any subject related to acting will be considered. Submissions and inquiries will be acknowledged immediately. Articles will be anonymously peer-reviewed. The MLA Style format is required. There are no length requirements or limitations.

We also seek book reviewers; contact Dr. Charles Grimes at grimesc@uncw.edu for a list of titles for review.

Email Senior Editor Dr. Ruis Woertendyke at rwoertendyke@pace.edu with requests for more information, proposals, abstracts, or submissions. If you're interested in becoming part of the Editorial Board, contact rwoertendyke@pace.edu. or grimesc@uncw.edu.

Abstracts for Volume 4 Due   1/15/18
Articles Due   5/10/18

Colophon

This third edition of *Methods: A Journal of Acting Pedagogy*
was published in Fall 2017
by Pace University Press

Cover and Interior Design by Sara Yager assisted by Mary Katherine Cornfield
The journal was typeset in Minion Pro and Myriad Pro
and printed by Lighting Source in La Vergne, Tennessee

Pace University Press
Director: Sherman Raskin
Associate Director: Manuela Soares
Graduate Assistants: Bryan Potts and Ellian Mellet
Student Aide: Erica Magrin

www.ingramcontent.com/pod-product-compliance
Lightning Source LLC
Chambersburg PA
CBHW061446300426
44114CB00014B/1864